Historic Brentwood

Historic Brentwood

VANCE LITTLE
Photographs by DOUG BRACHEY

JM Publications
A Division Of
JM PRODUCTIONS
BRENTWOOD, TN 37027

ISBN: 0-939298-51-1

PRINTED IN THE UNITED STATES OF AMERICA

First Edition

Contents

Publisher's Note 7

Introduction 9

1. Indians of Brentwood 11
2. Early Explorers and Settlers 18
3. Early Settlements in Middle Tennessee 21
4. Brentwood in the Harpeth Valley 27
5. Historic Families and Homes 32
6. Civil War Brentwood 86
7. Historic Schools 92
8. Historic Churches 94
9. Transportation and Communication 105
10. Maryland Farms 116
11. The Renaissance 121
12. Historic Businesses 127
13. City Government 138

Appendix A: Collin McDaniel 144
Appendix B: Gone to Texas 148
Appendix C: The Nightclub Era 151
Appendix D: Boy Scout Troop #1 152
Index 153

In Memory
of
Mary Sneed Jones

Publisher's Note

Everyone who lives during a notable or historic era contributes in some way to its making. There are notable people who receive publicity and recognition, and there are also others who are less well-known, who, nevertheless, influence the shaping of that era. Obviously, it would be impossible to mention by name all the people who have "lived" the history captured in this book. However, their contributions, whether great or small, deserve to be acknowledged. History is nothing more than a chronicle of the people who lived it in the making. Although this book focuses on the Brentwood community, in the larger sense it is a celebration of Brentwood's colorful background and of the people who made it so. Whether famous or obscure, all of Brentwood's residents over the years have left their mark on the town.

After history is made, it becomes the task of succeeding generations to preserve that history and pass it on to future generations, and this has been our motivation in publishing *Historic Brentwood*. Collecting, assimilating, and publishing "raw" information is no easy task: it takes a concerted effort and painstaking cooperation, and often it is not possible to reconstruct the past with as much accuracy as is desirable. Nonetheless, we are proud of our efforts, and hope you will find this book both entertaining and informative.

Vance Little, the book's author, deserves special recognition not only for his patient cooperation in the project, but also for the vast range of knowledge he carefully accumulated through the years as he sought Brentwood's "roots."

Doug Brachey, our photographer, took many days of his valuable time away from his business to make and develop the photographs. For his concerted efforts and hard work, we express our thanks.

Glenn Huff, Glenn Noble, John Sloan, Jr., Calvin Houghland, Jr., and the Pewitt family deserve mention for their first-hand accounts of Brentwood's recent past, which they gladly shared with the author and publishers.

A special word of thanks is due to Virginia Bowman, Williamson County historian, who, upon examining the manuscript, made valuable suggestions to improve its accuracy and kindly consented to write the book's introduction.

We wish to express our sincere appreciation to Maryland Farms for the financial assistance that made this project possible.

We hope that the publication of *Historic Brentwood* will be welcomed as an historic event in its own right. Our desire in making *Historic Brentwood* has been the creation of a unique volume which every resident of Brentwood will be proud to keep and to show to friends with the prideful statement, "This is where I live."

Introduction

Until now, there was no comprehensive history of Brentwood. Its past and swiftly-moving present was a story waiting to be told. Williamson Countians, and Brentwood residents in particular, are fortunate that Vance Little has written this beautiful book on Brentwood.

New-comers to the area are always fascinated by the landmarks which local people have always taken for granted. To see Brentwood's old homes and churches is to know that there is a rich heritage behind them, and many want to know what that heritage is.

The answer can be found in *Historic Brentwood.* In its pages, Mr. Little leads the reader from Indian days to modern times. Through his facile pen, we see the Red Man's old stone graves, an ancient explorer's tree carvings, and the white settlers' struggle to tame a hostile land.

We can visit the old homes and meet the families who built them, for Brentwood was fortunate in having many remarkable founding families whose strength was passed to several generations. Only in recent years has this bonding been weakened by several contributing factors.

Still standing are some of the same old meeting houses where the stalwarts of the faith held forth over a century ago. The modern congregation's singing echoes against the same walls as did their ancestor's voices.

There are too many topics in this book to cover in a brief introduction, but a glimpse at its pages reveals the magnitude of research involved in its writing.

Mr. Little is eminently qualified for such an enterprise. A lifelong interest in history inspired by his parents led to his association with many historical organizations, both local and state-wide.

The author holds membership in Historical Nashville Incorporated, the Tennessee Historical Society, the Rutherford County Historical Society, and the Sons of Confederate Veterans. He is vice-president and past president of the Williamson County Historical Society, past director and vice-president of the Heritage Foundation of Franklin and Williamson County, past vice-chairman of the Tennessee State Museum Association, and past president and director of the Carnton Association. He was a director of the Middle Tennessee Electric Membership Corporation, the Williamson County Farm Bureau, and the Liberty Bank of Brentwood and Franklin. These memberships are in addition to the civic and business organizations which demand his time.

Mr. Little is a lecturer and writer of note on historical and genealogical subjects, besides teaching in his chosen avocation of banking and law. He frequently serves as editor or co-editor of the Williamson County Historical Society Publication, and has written many articles on a variety of subjects.

In 1977, Mr. Little was recipient of the Patron Award presented by the Heritage Foundation for excellence in the preservation of local history.

In 1983, he was made an honorary member of Franklin Chapter No. 14, United Daughters of the Confederacy, for his generosity in providing legal work in their behalf. The Daughters awarded him the Jefferson Davis Medal, given for excellence in the preservation of Southern history.

Historic Brentwood does not dwell altogether on the long ago. The community's immediate past and its present struggles to cope with expanding growth are detailed. The section on Maryland Farms, what it was and what it has become, is typical of those explanations. The many fine photographs throughout the book add beauty and interest.

Horse lovers will enjoy reading about Maryland Farms' American Ace, the Iroquois Steeplechase, and the other notable equines mentioned.

Our fondness for books written about people and places we have loved never diminishes. They grow dearer as the years pass into the ages, and in that tradition *Historic Brentwood* will be cherished by lifelong residents of Middle Tennessee, by new-comers to the area, and by those who are yet to know and appreciate Brentwood.

Virginia McDaniel Bowman
October 4, 1985

1
Indians Of Brentwood

The Shawnee

When the first settlers came to the Brentwood area, they found it relatively free of Indians. At that time, no Indians actually lived in the Great Central Basin of Middle Tennessee. Indians had lived in the area in years past, and several tribes concurrently claimed right to the rich valleys of the Central Basin.

The Shawnee tribes inhabited the Central Basin of Tennessee before the arrival of the White settlers. They had several villages throughout the Central Basin and Cumberland Valley, perhaps one or more in the Brentwood area.

There are numerous accounts of trade with the Shawnee Indians during the late 1600's and early 1700's, especially by the French. One such French trader was Martin Chartier who lived with the Shawnee and traded with them in the late 1600's. By the mid 1700's, the Shawnee were gone from the Central Basin, having been driven out by neighboring Chickasaw and Cherokee. The expulsion of the Shawnee left the Middle Tennessee area a "no man's land", but a prize that the various tribes of Indians, namely the Cherokee, Chickasaw, Chickamauga, and Choctaw were willing to share for hunting and fishing purposes.

The Central Basin of Tennessee may have been a no man's land at the time of the arrival of the settlers, but it had not always been so. Those first settlers found evidence of previous inhabitants and cultures. They found man-made structures such as the Boiling Springs Mounds on what is now Moores Lane in Brentwood that attested to a prior culture.

The Mound Builders

The Mound Builders lived in the Brentwood area perhaps 2,000 years ago. They were possibly descended from earlier Indian tribes, the earliest of whom were the Paleolithic (Old Stone Age) tribes, who were wandering hunters. Thousands of years ago, possibly as many as 100,000 years, they came out of Asia, crossed the Bering Strait and fanned out across the Americas, possibly in front of an advancing Ice Age.

The earliest nomadic Indians were most noted for their fluted spear points which they have left as a testimony to their presence in the local area. These spear points, known as "Clovis points," were made from chipped flint and have been found in several Middle Tennessee counties. These people were hunters and fishers without permanent home sites. They lived in small bands of around 25 people. The men hunted and made tools and weapons, while the women took care of the children, made clothes, gathered wood and plants, and cooked.

As the ice of the Ice Age receded, the weather moderated, and plants began to grow. The Indians began to lead a more settled existence and built for themselves more substantial homes — more substantial than the temporary lean-to's of their ancestors.

The Indians of Brentwood thus entered the Mesolithic Period, or the Archaic Period. They still hunted and fished, but they set up semi-permanent residence in caves and crude huts. They are known as "the gatherers." These Indians spread throughout America and lived thusly for thousands of years. Some continued this life style in isolated areas until the coming of the White Man. They became more adept at using the spear and expanded their diets to include shellfish, nuts, greens, and berries. They began to weave and make simple unadorned pottery.

"Brentwood has a fine example of the Mound Builders' craft in the Boiling Springs Mound on Moores Lane."

The immediate ancestors of the Indians who left the most indelible mark, their mounds, on Brentwood were the Neolithic Indians or Early Woodland Indians. They domesticated plants and animals and lived in small villages in circular huts. Their culture advanced to the stage to include arts and crafts. Their villages were larger and more permanent although tribes had not yet formed. They learned the use of the bow and arrow. Their weaving and potting became more advanced. They began to trade with Indians in other parts of the country. In these people, we see the first emergence of religion. In the burying of their dead, they prepared them for an afterlife, placing in their tombs decorated pottery and other artifacts. They buried their dead on top of the ground and covered them with dirt. The next to die was placed on top of the last and covered. Hence, their burial practices gave rise to the burial mounds, which became prominent in a later period.

The Woodland Period gave way to the "golden age" of the Indians of the Brentwood area. This golden age is called the Mississippian Period. The Indians of this period became the Mound Builders and the Stone Box Grave Indians. At the height of this civilization, the Little Harpeth Valley was perhaps as heavily populated as it is today.

Boiling Springs Mound yielded numerous Indian artifacts.

The Mound Builders also lived in other areas of Williamson County. They had towns located on the Lewisburg Pike three miles out of Franklin, known as the DeGraffenreid Site, at Old Town on Natchez Trace and a site on the Del Rio Pike. They lived in fortified towns on streams and built mounds, perhaps for religious reasons. These mounds were built by carrying dirt in baskets and piling basket load on top of basket load. Some mounds were burial mounds and others were for ceremonial purposes. Evidence of fires has been found, the ashes from which were covered with new dirt.

Brentwood has a fine example of the Mound Builders' craft in the Boiling Spring Mound on Moores Lane. This mound, also called the Fewkes Site, named for E. W. Fewkes who led the exploration in 1920, originally consisted of some 15 acres. Like other Mound Builders' towns, this site was located near a stream and several springs that form the head water of the Little Harpeth River. There were originally several mounds at this site. All except the largest, which was the ceremonial mound, were excavated in the 1920 dig. Many items of interest, including vases and idols, were found.

For the most part, the Mound Builders located their towns in areas of rich soil, near streams that were a source of water as well as a natural fortification. There were extensive earthworks on the sides of their towns which were not bordered by rivers, streams, or other natural fortifications.

"The Mound Builders and their culture mysteriously disappeared from Brentwood and the Middle Tennessee area before the first explorers came into the area."

The mounds in the town sites varied in number and dimension. The smallest were only a few feet high and 30 or so feet in diameter. The largest on the other hand, ranged up to 70 feet high and covered up to two acres of land. The largest of the mounds, such as the Boiling Springs Mound, are called pyramidal mounds and were probably sites of temples or council houses.

The mounds were built in clusters around a large plaza. In the flat area the people gathered for religious ceremonies, games, or other public activities. Some of the towns had 200 to 300 houses, and up to 2,000 residents. A wooden palisade was built on the sides of the towns that did not have natural fortifications. Farming was done outside the fence where they grew corn, squash, pumpkin, and beans. The Indians also made fine pottery and jewelry.

In addition to the spectacular temple mound on Moores Lane, many burial mounds have been found in the Brentwood area. Extensive stone box graves have been found on the Brentwood Country Club property as well as neighboring Meadow Lake Subdivision. Burial mounds have also been found on Kelly road and near Traveler's Rest.

Boiling Springs Mound
on Moores Lane.

Recognized archaeologists and Indian authorities such as William Edward Myer and Gates P. Thurston have stated that some of the most significant remains of prehistoric Indian civilizations are to be found within a 30 mile radius of Nashville. This area is the richest in such sites in the Southeastern United States. Nashville served as a focal point for Mound Builder villages located in what are now surrounding counties of Middle Tennessee, including Williamson County.

Old roads and Indian trails connected the towns of the Mound Builders. One such Indian trail ran east of Wilson Pike crossing Old Smyrna Road at the Frost Place. The trail continued on to the Boiling Springs site on Moores Lane and then on to the so-called DeGraffenreid Site, located on the Lewisburg Pike, southeast of Franklin.

The Mound Builders and their culture mysteriously disappeared from Brentwood and the Middle Tennessee area before the first explorers came into the area in the 1500's. These explorers, who included DeSoto and his Spanish entourage as well as French hunters and traders, mentioned having found abandoned forts; but none of them mentioned the people who built and lived in these forts. We can only assume that the Mound Builders were wiped out by war, pestilence, or famine, or possibly migrated to Mexico and Central America to join the Aztec and the Mayan. The latter is a possibility since the civilization of the Middle Tennessee Mound Builders was a crude and rustic version of the more advanced civilization of the Aztec and Mayan.

The Owl Creek People

Local Indian authority Malcolm Parker has stated that more pre-historic Indian artifacts have been found in Tennessee than any other state in the Union. He goes on to say that the Cumberland country of Middle Tennessee must have been their "Garden of Eden." He further states that Williamson County must have been a favorite corner in that garden.

The Owl Creek site is located just off Concord Road near the confluence of Mill Creek and Owl Creek, about three miles outside the city limits of Brentwood. This site was discovered in 1972 and excavated during the following two years. The results of this excavation revealed that the Indians who lived at the site were primarily of the Mesolithic Period, also called Archaic Period and early Woodland Period. The several styles of tools and weapons unearthed indicated that the Owl Creek site was occupied as early as 6,000 B.C.

The Owl Creek People were hunters and gatherers. Their garbage found near

"The Owl Creek site is located just off Concord Road . . . about three miles outside the city limits."

the "kitchen" area of the site suggested a diet of primarily mussels, supplemented by fish, turtle, and water snails taken from the Owl and Mill Creeks. Diets also included such wildlife as turkey, deer, and beaver, which was theirs for the taking. Their debris indicates that acorns and hazelnuts were also eaten in abundance. Remnants of charcoal are evidence that they cooked their food over open fires.

The Owl Creek People used the bow and arrow as well as the atlatl, a throwing device attached to spears. Many flint projectiles, knife blades, and scrapers were also found at the site. No less than 300 limestone hammers and pestles were found. There was evidence that after roasted deer was eaten, the Owl Creek People would split the bones and eat the marrow for dessert.

A large number of polished bone awls, flakers, and needles were found, as well as grooved sandstone whet stones and abraders. No ornaments of shell, stone or bone were found, nor was there any form of agriculture. These arts were for a later generation.

Evidence at the Owl Creek Site indicated that these people lived in lean-to huts and shelters. Post moulds at 45 degree angles were found. The dead were buried in the earth in a flexed position, that is, the knees were drawn up under the chin. Caches of flint knife blades and spearheads were buried with the dead. Some stone box graves were found at Owl Creek indicating that the site was also inhabited by Indians of a later period, perhaps as recent as 1,000 A.D.

The Historic Period

With the passing of the Mound Builders, the Indians seemed to pass into a period of cultural regression or dark ages. The Indians of the Historic Period, whom the White Settlers found as they migrated westward, had more of the customs and characteristics of the Woodland Period, which pre-dated the Mound Builders. They hunted and fished, and seem to have lost the sophisticated social structure of their predecessors.

"The two tribes that had the most influence on the Middle Tennessee area were the Chickasaw and the Cherokee."

The Indians of the Historic Period in Tennessee included such familiar names as Shawnee, Cherokee, Chickasaw, Chickamauga, and Chocktaw. The Shawnee, who were driven out of the Central Basin in the mid-1700's, and who were known for their propensity to cover great distances, migrated to Ohio. They were also found in Maryland and Pennsylvania. They later terrorized the Northwest, and were always known for their hatred of the White Man.

The two Indian tribes that had the most influence on the Middle Tennessee area were the Chickasaw and the Cherokee. The Chickasaw lived west of the Tennessee River were related to the Chocktaw tribe of North Mississippi. The Chocktaw were settled farmers, while their Chickasaw cousins were warriors.

The Cherokee lived in East Tennessee, the Carolinas, and North Georgia. They had a long history of conflict with the White Man, particularly the Wautauga Settlement in East Tennessee.

2
Early Explorers And Settlers

Hernando DeSoto

Hunters and explorers were in the Middle Tennessee area several hundred years before the first permanent settlers arrived. The most famous of these explorers to touch the soil of Tennessee was DeSoto. It is not likely, however, that he was the first. There is evidence that the Indians had been exposed to the ways of the White Man before the arrival of DeSoto, particularly his diseases. Tradition suggests that great numbers of Indians had succumbed to epidemics brought by early settlers. The visitation of such a pestilence could explain the disappearance of the Mississippi Mound Builders and their culture.

In any event, DeSoto landed in Florida in 1539. He brought ashore near Tampa Bay some 600 soldiers in full military regalia who represented the best of Spanish noble families. They were supported by 220 horses and a retinue of servants and slaves in addition to 24 priests and monks who were brought along to convert the savages to Christianity. DeSoto's army also included pigs, mules, and a pack of vicious bloodhounds.

DeSoto and his army moved inland in search of gold and riches. He had little sympathy with or mercy upon the Indians whom he met along the way. His cruelty to the natives laid the ground work for generations of conflict between the Red Men and the White Men.

"DeSoto and his army had little sympathy with or mercy upon the Indians."

Records establish that DeSoto and his men approached Middle Tennessee. Such records, however, do not reveal that they were ever in the Brentwood area. But a local phenomenon has raised some interesting speculation. On the George

Washington Carmichael Herbert farm on Old Smyrna Road there is a beech tree that bears the date of 1563. The date on the tree, which is located on the Old South Indian Trail, is still visible and quite distinct. The date is a few years off, but maybe some stragglers from the DeSoto party passed this way.

The tree also bears other dates and names, in keeping with the custom in years past of carving names and dates on trees. If the trees were full grown the carvings would never be any higher from the ground when carved, and the carvings would grow as the tree grew. One of the carvings on the Herbert tree near the date in question is indistinct, but it appears to be a name beginning with "le" or "la," which would indicate a French carver. This speculation raises another interesting possibility.

The French Traders

French traders and explorers were known to be in the Middle Tennessee area in the late 1600's, if not before. A Frenchman by the name of Martin Chartier is known to have been in the Nashville area in the 1680's. He lived with the Shawnee Indians, having deserted LaSalle's army in Canada and taking residence with the Shawnees in Illinois and later moving to Tennessee with them.

Another Frenchman named Jean du Charleville had a trading post near what is now Fifth Avenue North and Jefferson Street in Nashville in the second decade of the 1700's. The group of log cabins at Sevier Park on Granny White Pike is said to date to French traders in the 1700's.

Daniel Boone

Inevitably, stories of rich soils, hardwood forests, and lush strands of blue grass reached the residents of the seaboard colonies. Explorers were sent to scout the area. One of the first and most famous was Daniel Boone. He traveled into Tennessee and Kentucky, where along with his other accomplishments, he "cilled a bar" and memorialized that fact in the bark of a tree. Apparently his exploring was better than his spelling because excitement about the land beyond the mountains continued to build in the eastern colonies.

The James Smith Party

In June 1766, a party set out from the East to explore the Valley of the Cumberland and other points west. This party, headed by Colonel James Smith, included Joshua Horton, Uriah Stone, William Baker, and a slave belonging to Horton. On this journey, Uriah Stone gave his name to Stones River. Glowing reports of rich soils, plants, and animal life were given on their return home.

The Uriah Stone Party

Again in 1770 Uriah Stone and others, including Casper Mansker, John Baker, Thomas Gordon, Humphrey Hogan, and Cadi Brook, built two boats and descended the Cumberland River, which was probably the first trade in that stream. At the French Lick, now Nashville, they found immense numbers of buffalo and other wild game. Near the lick they found the fort built by the French for trade with the Indians. Several of these scouts came back as permanent settlers on the Cumberland.

3
Early Settlements In Middle Tennessee

Middle Tennessee was officially settled in 1780 when two groups of settlers arrived on the banks of the Cumberland at what is now Nashville. One group came by land and the other by water. Both groups left Wautauga settlement in upper East Tennessee. The spring before their departure, a small party led by James Robertson had come out from Wautauga to the Cumberland site to build cabins and plant a crop in anticipation of the arrival of permanent settlers the next year.

The James Robertson Party

The two parties left Fort Patrick Henry on the Holston River in 1779. Robertson led a band of men with their livestock that took a circuitous route through the Cumberland Gap, through Kentucky, then south to the Great Salt Lick. The weather was bitterly cold, and game was scarce. Robertson and his men arrived at the site of Nashville on Christmas Day 1779 in a greatly emaciated and famished condition. They found the Cumberland River frozen solid. So thick was the ice that they, along with their livestock, were able to cross on the ice to the south bank of the river.

The John Donelson Party

The other party of women and children was led by John Donelson. A flotilla of boats left Fort Patrick Henry on December 22, 1779. It was a four months journey fraught with danger at every turn of the river. The clumsy handmade rafts were ill equipped to navigate the shoals and sucks encountered along the way. Boats were wrecked in the shallow waters. Colonel Hutchings' slave suffered frostbite from the bitter cold. Ephraim Peyton's wife gave birth to a baby. A young Mr. Payne died from injuries received when a boat ran too near the shore. Smallpox broke out on the Stewart boat, which was captured by Indians and all aboard were murdered. At a narrow point in the river the party was attacked by Indians. The boat of Jonathan Jennings was caught in the Whirl and had to be left behind. The passengers escaped and later rejoined the flotilla. With great difficulty, the fleet negotiated the dreaded Muscle Shoals amid the deafening roar. The rag tag group of boats continued on the Tennessee River to the Ohio, then to the Cumberland, fighting the current until they reached their friends, husbands, and fathers awaiting them at the Great Salt Lick.

The Earliest Settlers

The Donelson and Robertson groups who arrived at Nashboro in the winter of 1779-1780 are generally credited with being the first settlers in Middle Tennessee and were the beginning of what is now Nashville. The area was already well known to explorers and hunters before the settlers arrived. Actually, there were some few settlers who had located in the area of the Great Salt Lick before Donelson and Robertson arrived on the scene.

The Williams family, long prominent in Brentwood, was one who preceded Donelson and Robertson. Their property was on Cloverland Drive and included Cloverland Estates and Saddlewood subdivision.

Daniel Williams, born in Hanover County, Virginia, in the 1720's, moved to South Carolina and later to Middle Tennessee with his family. They arrived in the company of John Rice, who became a wealthy Nashville merchant and landowner. Williams died in Davidson County in 1793, leaving several children.

Daniel Williams' son, Nimrod, located on land near Brentwood. His descendants still own and live on a part of this land. The family cemetery is located behind a house in Saddlewood subdivision.

"After their arrival at Nashboro, the first settlers put the finishing touches on the fort that had begun the prior year."

After their arrival at Nashboro, the first settlers put the finishing touches on the fort that had begun the prior year when the scouting party had come to the site and planted corn. It had been a severe winter, and game and plants were scarce. They were literally alone in the wilderness — without food, clothing, or shelter, and without formal government and protection. By their industry they took care of the necessities and formed their own government, called the Cumberland Compact. Of the men who signed the document, only one had to use a mark: the others all were able to sign their names, which was a real tribute to the educational level of these frontiersmen.

It was the lack of protection from Indian attack that almost caused the failure of the struggling settlement. Successive and continued Indian attacks over the first 10 years caused many of the settlers to forsake the settlement and flee to safety in Kentucky, Illinois, or Natchez. Only the most stalwart stayed, following the example of James Robertson, whose leadership was instrumental in the success of the settlement at Nashboro.

The reasons for the incessant Indian attacks were complex, and did not occur solely because the Whites had taken over Indian land. Few Indians actually lived in the Middle Tennessee area. They claimed hunting rights, but no rights of domicile. Therefore, there had to be something more behind the hatred of the Red Man than an invasion of his homeland.

The answer to the ferocity of the Indians can be found in a review of their relations with the White Man since days of exploration. DeSoto came armed with swords rather than plowshares. The Indians had long memories, and subsequent generations of Southeastern Indians were imbued with a deep prejudice against the White Man.

The settlers of the Eastern colonies had little problem with the Indians.

Basically, the settlers of the Eastern colonies who came armed with plowshares had little problem with the Indians. Much has been said about cooperation between the two races and how they helped each other.

The real conflict between the Indians and British settlers came as a result of problems that had their origin in Europe. British and French claims in North America culminated in the French and Indian War. The animosity of the Indians came from the influence of the French and their incitement of the Indians against the English settlers.

The same was true in the Southeast, except that it was the Spanish who had designs on the Southeastern territory. They incited the Indians to attack the new settlements on the Cumberland. The attacks of the Creek Indians on the settlements is a specific example of such instigation. These Indians were residents of Georgia, and were in no way threatened by the Cumberland Settlement.

The British also had a hand in the Indian uprisings. When the settlers arrived on the Cumberland, the Revolutionary War was raging in the East. Many of the Cumberland settlers were veterans of the Battle of Kings Mountain. The British had enlisted the support of the Indians to help subjugate the rebellious American colonies.

For whatever reasons, the Indians manifested antagonism with raids on the Cumberland settlers for a period of ten or more years. No family was spared these atrocities. Men, women, and children fell victims to the tomahawk.

Indian Attacks at Mayfield Station

In their first year at the Cumberland settlement many people lost their lives at the hands of the Indians. One such person was James Mayfield, who was killed at Eaton's Station, the present site of the Werthan Bag Company located on what is now Eight Avenue North. After his death, his heirs received a grant from the State of North Carolina for 640 acres on the "headwaters of the West Fort of Mill Creek." Presumably, this was the land upon which Mayfield's Station was later built.

Southerland Mayfield, a son of James Mayfield, took up the grant, and his family became the first white people in the Brentwood area. They built a fort for the protection of themselves and their neighbors. The Mayfield land was 640 acres located on the northeast corner of Old Smyrna Road and Wilson Pike. At least one local historian places the site of this fort near the Frost home on Old Smyrna Road.

Southerland Mayfield was attacked by Creek Indians in 1788 at Mayfield's Station. A party of 10 to 12 warriors came upon Mayfield, his two sons, Berry Joslin and another man named Martin. They were building a wolf pen and had left their guns against a nearby tree. The Indians crept between the Mayfields and their guns. They shot Southerland Mayfield, his son William, and a man named Martin who had been hired to guard the station. The younger Mayfield and the soldier were killed and scalped by the Indians on the spot. Berry Joslin was able to escape by jumping over a log and scrambling into the forest. Southerland Mayfield was found by the family the next morning. He had died from wounds during the night. One of the sons, George, was taken captive by the Creek Indians and taken to Alabama, where he remained with the Indians for 12 years before making it back home to Brentwood. After the attack, Mrs. Mayfield moved the family to Rains Station for safety.

"George Mayfield was captured by the Indians, but returned to his home in Brentwood several years later."

In 1824 Berry Joslin, in connection with a lawsuit, made an affidavit concerning Mayfield's Station in which he stated that he, John Haggart, and John Campbell and their families went to live in Southerland Mayfield's Station just before the Indian attack. He stated that they had a contract with Mayfield to live there two years, and in exchange for this lodging they would clear two acres of land and each build a new station. Soon after they moved into the station, it was attacked and burned by the Indians. In his account of the attack, Joslin said they were burning logs to plant the first crop of corn when the Indians came and fired on them. He stated, "We were putting up a wolf pen about half a mile from the station. Southerland Mayfield and one Martin, a soldier, were killed. George Mayfield was taken prisoner and William Mayfield was also killed. We all in a few days left with Mrs. Mayfield at her request."

George Mayfield, the son who was taken captive, returned to his Brentwood home several years later. One version of his story says that he escaped from the Indians when they allowed him to go hunting alone. Another version says that his mother paid two hundred dollars for his ransom. After his return to Brentwood, he served as an interpreter and guide for Andrew Jackson during the Indian Wars and the War of 1812. He later married and became the father of Dr. Southerland Shannon Mayfield, a prominent physician in the Brentwood area for many years during the 1800's.

The Leiper Grant

Bittersweet memories are connected with the Leiper Grant in Brentwood. The recipient of this grant was Captain James Leiper, a bright star in the Cumberland settlement's cast of characters. He came from Kentucky and was one of the signers of the Cumberland Compact. In 1780, he was the bridegroom in the settlement's first wedding when he was married to Susan Drake. The ceremony was performed by Col. James Robertson himself. Their married life was cut short, however, when Captain Leiper was killed in an Indian raid on Fort Nashboro scarcely six months after the wedding. This raid was the famous attack during which Charlotte Robertson unleashed a pack of dogs on the Indians, routing them from the fort.

"Susan Drake Leiper met an untimely death when she accidentally knocked a loaded gun from its rack over the door. It discharged, killing her instantly."

After the death of her husband, Susan Drake Leiper gave birth to a daughter whom she named Sarah Jane. While the child was still an infant, Mrs. Leiper, herself then only twenty years of age, met an untimely death when she accidentally knocked a loaded gun from its rack over the door. It discharged, killing her instantly.

The Leipers' daughter inherited the 640-acre grant, which was awarded posthumously to her father. It was located in Brentwood in what is now the Lipscomb-Concord Road area.

In 1798, Sarah Jane Leiper married Alexander Smith, and they came to live on her Brentwood grant. Alexander Smith was the son of Robert and Sarah Clemmons Smith. His mother died in 1809 and was the first person buried in the Hightower Cemetery in what is now Carondelet subdivision on Wilson Pike. His sister Nancy (1770-1826) married Richard Hightower. Their home was the manor house of the plantation that is now Carondelet. The Hightowers were equally as prominent in early Brentwood days as were the Alexander Smiths. Their daughter Sarah Clemmons Hightower married Oliver Bliss Hayes, and they became the parents of Adelicia Hayes Acklen, builder of Belmont and certainly Nashville's most colorful character in the mid-1800's.

Alexander Smith was a surveyor and was one of the three commissioners appointed to represent Tennessee in the settlement of the boundary dispute with North Carolina. On their land they had a meal and flour mill as well as a furniture factory. A son of the Smiths, Benjamin Drake Smith, became a lawyer and later a Presbyterian minister.

In his will, Alexander Smith states that it was his primary object to provide for his wife Sarah Leiper Smith, "in whom I have the most implicit confidence and to whose discretion I trust the disposition of all property which I have given her . . ." He also stated in his will that he had already given 200 acres to his daughter Elizabeth C. Hadley, wife of Denny Porterfield Hadley, on which they built Green Pastures (now the beautiful Franklin Road home of Mr. and Mrs. Jesse Henley). He further stated that he had given to his daughter Emeline Christmas, wife of Richard Christmas, 200 acres of land and 21 acres of corn in lieu of a slave. Upon this site they built Ashlawn, which at this writing is the magnificent Oman home on Franklin Road.

4
Brentwood In The Harpeth Valley

Origin of the Name "Harpeth"

Brentwood is located in the heart of a valley drained by the Little Harpeth River. The name "Harpeth" has existed for many years, but its origins have been obscured by the passage of time.

The Little Harpeth River is a tributary of the Harpeth River, which drains a basin of about 895 square miles. Rising in southwest Rutherford County, the Harpeth River meanders in a generally northwest direction through Williamson, Davidson, and Cheatham Counties. This waterway is fed by the tributaries of South Harpeth, West Harpeth, and Little Harpeth Rivers. The Harpeth extends for 118 miles through Middle Tennessee before its confluence with the Cumberland River near Ashland City.

One of the earliest descriptions of the Harpeth River is in the works of surveyor Thomas Hutchins. In 1768 he labeled the stream "Fish Creek," which was used until the 1780's when the name "Harpath" began to appear on maps. The spelling was later standardized to the current name of Harpeth.

One explanation of the name's origin contends that the name came from two celebrated highwaymen named for their sizes, Big Harp and Little Harp. They headquartered themselves on the Harpeth River, terrorizing settlers from far and near, and were especially active on the Old Natchez Trace. Disguised as itinerant preachers, they would gain the confidence of their victims before robbing and murdering them. Eventually, Big Harp was captured and decapitated, and his head was placed upon a pole where the road crosses a creek at a place still known as Harp's Head. Little Harp was later captured and executed at Washington, Mississippi. Though fascinating and colorful, it seems unlikely that these highwaymen are the source of the name "Harpeth."

A better explanation came from the late historian Edward W. Hicks, lifelong resident of Devon Farm on the Harpeth River. In a speech before the Tennessee Historical Society in 1892, he claimed that the name comes from *The Spectator*, a popular periodical in London in the 1700's. In a 1714 edition, its editor Joseph Addison tells of an Oriental legend concerning two brothers, Harpath and Shalum, who became rivals for the affection of a beautiful woman named Hilpa. When Harpath was victorious over his brother in winning the maiden's hand, Shalum cursed him and prayed for a mountain to fall on him. Harpath fearfully avoided mountains from that day forward, but eventually drowned by accident in a river issuing from a mountain. The river was named Harpath in his memory.

Origin of the Name "Brentwood"

There has been much speculation about the origin of the name "Brentwood," but nothing definite has ever been concluded. There are several theories of how the town was named. Some have opined that it came from a corruption of the term "break for wood" since Brentwood was the first stop for wood for trains leaving Nashville. However, this theory seems unlikely since the post office was using the name Brentwood before the trains came.

Another theory is that the name comes from the term "burnt wood," and may be named for an English town called Brentwood. It is true that there is such a town north of London which traces its name back to the expression "burnt wood," which resulted from an ancient disaster in the area. There is no evident connection between the English town of Brentwood and the Tennessee community of the same name.

Another theory of the origin of the name Brentwood is that it comes from Brentwood, Maryland. One long-time Brentwood resident says that the head engineer overseeing the first railroad cut in the 1850's was from Brentwood, Maryland, and that he named the site of the railroad cut for his home town. Another life-long Brentwood resident comes to the same conclusion, but by a different route. He says that Brentwood takes its name from Brentwood, Maryland, because so many of the early settlers came from the Brentwood, Maryland area and brought the name with them.

The best explanation of the origin of the name "Brentwood" comes from Brentwood historian Richard Fulcher, who contends that the town took its name from the home of Horatio McNish, who named his home Brentwood after two ancestral homes in Virginia named Woodstock and Brenton. Research reveals that the family of Horatio McNish did in fact live in the Brentwood area from 1827 until the 1850's. McNish bought 320 acres from Henry R. Bachman and later sold a part of that land to Robert I. Moore. He is said to have built a two-story Colonial home on a hill just off Franklin Road "where he lived and raised a large family." McNish's mother, Elizabeth Lewis, claimed descent from the Tidewater Virginia family of

Brent and owned the estates referred to above. There is no evidence to date that McNish actually named his home Brentwood, but it is entirely plausible and seems the best explanation for origin of Brentwood's name.

The Town of Brentwood

Records indicate that the first "official" use of the name Brentwood was in 1856, when the post office was moved from Good Spring to Brentwood. The former location was on Wilson Pike at Old Smyrna Road. It is likely that the town of Brentwood, or what is known today as the town center, dates from the coming of the railroad in the 1850's.

"Brentwood probably took its name from Brenton and Woodstock, ancestral homes of Horatio McNish."

When the railroad was built, a cut was made, although it was not nearly so deep as the one made when the second railroad came in the early 1900's. The first cut required labor and housing. It has been speculated that Brentwood owes its beginning to being a camp for Irish laborers working on the railroad. In any event, the point where the two major roads, the Harpeth Turnpike and the Franklin Pike, converged, plus a railroad, had all the makings for a new town. The first railroad station was located on Church Street near the old post office building.

Williamson County civil districts were formed in 1836. The 15th Civil District became what is the City of Brentwood today. Horatio McNish was the first member of the County Court from the 15th District. The first constable was Robert A. Reed. Voting took place at the home of Alexander Smith.

In 1874, Dr. W. M. Clark wrote a description of Williamson County. In characterizing Brentwood, he said that it "boasts a woolen mill which bids fair to supply the needs of the county with all woolen fabricks." He further said that the mill belonged to "Mssrs. Holt, Gibbons, and Humphrey" and that "by next season they will have up all their machinery, already purchased, to manufacture jeans, blankets, flannels, etc. in as good style and as cheaply as can be produced elsewhere." Dr. Clark also said that William Davis had a "fine flour mill" near Brentwood. In 1875, the Williamson County *Review and Journal* carried the following notice:

> Brentwood Woolen Mills, J.P. Humphries and R.I. Moore, Jeans, Lindseys and other woolen goods, have machinery in fine order and prepared to cord wool.

In 1873, Brentwood was described as a "post station" in Williamson County. By 1881, the population had risen to 300, with a list of four business persons who operated two saloons, a woolen mill, a dry goods store, and a general store. In 1886, Brentwood was described as a station on the L&N Railroad near the county line, "beautifully situated" with several business houses, a post office, several shops, and a Methodist Church.

Stone Fences

If good fences make good neighbors, Brentwood must have been a community of good neighbors in the past. Stone fences abound in this community. However, those that are still standing are only a part of the original ones. Some were destroyed when it became necessary to widen highways to handle the traffic. With each road improvement, stone fences on one side of the road (if not both) usually have to be torn down.

Some people refer to the stone fences as slave walls, contending that they were built by slaves during the winter when there was no farming to be done. Local

Maple Lawn

Maple Lawn was built by Nathan and Jane Hightower Owen in the 1830's on a 300-acre tract of land that was an original land grant to John Cockrill. It was remodeled in the 1870's, giving it the present Victorian look.

Mooreland

Mooreland is built on land that was a Revolutionary War grant to General Robert Irvin. The house was begun in 1838 by their son Robert Irvin Moore. He died during the time the house was being built. It was completed on a less grand scale than Robert Irvin Moore had planned, which accounts for the off-center doors. Built in pure Greek Revival style, the house contains 22 rooms and a full basement where house servants lived. Part of the original metal roof, which came from England, is still in place. The house was used by both Confederate and Federal forces as a hospital during the Civil War. It was occupied by the Moore family until 1944.

Forge Seat

Forge Seat was built in 1808 by Samuel Crockett on land granted to his father, Revolutionary War veteran Andrew Crockett. It is built of brick laid in Flemish bond, and the interior resembles Independence Hall in Philadelphia. Built before the central hall came into vogue, each room has a staircase that leads to the room above. The Crocketts operated an iron forge on this site, and Andrew Jackson stopped at Forge Seat to purchase arms for his men en route to New Orleans during the War of 1812. A few rifles manufactured here still exist, and may be identified by S&AC engraved on the barrel.

Century Oak

Century Oak was built in the 1840's by James Hazard Wilson II for his son Samuel Wilson and his wife Lucy Ann Marshall. The house was originally a three story structure with twin chimneys, tied together with parapet walls extending over the roof. The present hip was added in the 1920's when the original roof was blown away in a storm.

Owen-Primm House

The Owen-Primm house was built by Jabez Owen, a member of a prominent early Brentwood family which had large land holdings and built several fine homes. It was built in the classic simplicity of a Middle Tennessee plantation house, with four columns supporting the two-story porch. The slave cabins are still intact along the drive leading to the rear of the house. The original log house is incorporated into the present house, and one log bears the date 1806.

40

McCrory House

Brentwood's oldest house is the McCrory House on the Davidson County side of Old Hickory Boulevard, just west of Granny White Pike. Built by Thomas McCrory in 1797, it is said to be the third oldest house still standing in Davidson County. It was used as a benchmark to describe the boundaries of Williamson County when it was formed out of Davidson County in 1799.

Midway

The original Midway was built in 1829 by Lysander McGavock, son of one of Nashville's earliest and most prominent settlers. It takes its name from being mid-way between Franklin and Nashville. The present structure was built in 1846 after a fire heavily damaged the original house. It was occupied by five generations of the McGavock descendants and leased in 1954 to the Brentwood Country Club.

Ravenswood

Ravenswood was built in 1825 by James Hazard Wilson II. It was named for Sam Houston, the first Governor of Texas, who was a friend of the Wilsons and was best man in James Hazard Wilson II's wedding.

Windy Hill

Windy Hill was built in the 1820's by Constantine Perkins and Susannah Hardeman Sneed. A ~~w~~ place may still be seen in the yard where the clay for bricks was dug. The house is ~~n~~structed over a large basement where valuables and even cows and horses were hidden ~~fr~~om Federal raiders during the Civil War.

Sneed Acres

James Sneed and his wife Bethenia Harden Perkins Sneed came to Brentwood in 1798 and
built the original log cabin which forms Sneed Acres.

Foxview

Foxview was built by Alexander Ewing Sneed, youngest child of pioneer James Sneed. He
had two sons who served in the Confederate Army. Foxview was bought by the Schwab
family, who extensively rebuilt and remodeled, using the old house as the central core of the
building.

47

Boxwood Hall

Boxwood Hall, situated on what is now Meadow Lake Subdivision, was built in 1852 by Emily McGavock Hayes and her husband, Oliver Bliss Hayes, Jr., on land given to her by her father, Lysander McGavock, builder of Midway. The lumber in the original part of the house came from trees cut on the property. The bricks were also made there.

Crockett Springs

Crockett Springs was built by Joseph
Crockett, who came to the Brentwood area
in 1808 to take up the 640 acres willed to
him by his father. Today the house forms
the central part of the clubhouse for
Crockett Springs National Golf and
Country Club. The photograph at the top
of the opposite page shows the house prior
to its renovation by Glenn Noble.

Knox-Crockett House

The Knox-Crockett House was built by Major Andrew Crockett, who settled here in 1799. Typical of early architecture, the house was originally two log rooms with a "dog trot."

Mountview

Mountview was built in the early 1860's by William A. and Judith Robertson Owen Davis. The columns rise in trim, tall lines, characteristic of pre-Civil War Tennessee plantation houses and was built from bricks made on location.

Isola Bella

Isola Bella was built around 1840 by James and Narcissa Merritt Johnston. The property originally belonged to David Johnston, grandfather of the builder. During the Civil War, the lawn of Isola Bella was traversed by both Confederate and Federal cannons, wagons, and marching soldiers.

Brentvale

Brentvale was built in 1830 by William Temple Sneed, seventh child of pioneer James Sneed.
It was built from huge logs cut on location.

Mayfield

Mayfield was the home of Southerland Mayfield, personal physician of Andrew Jackson. The Mayfields were the first white family in the Brentwood area. Arriving in 1790, they built a fort to protect themselves as well as other settlers to follow. Six members of the Mayfield family were killed by Indians, and one son, George, was kidnapped by the Creek Indians, who held him captive for 12 years.

Cotton Port

Cotton Port is one of the oldest brick houses in the Brentwood area. It was built shortly after the Frost family came here in 1811. The builders of the house were Captain John Frost and his wife Rhoda Miles Frost, who came to Tennessee from Newberry, South Carolina. John Frost was a Captain in the War of 1812. The Frost place was known in early times as Cotton Port. In the early 1800's, the post office was located there, as well as the general store, cotton mill, and grist mill.

Ashlawn

Ashlawn was built in the 1830's by Richard and Mary Ann Smith Christmas. The walls of handmade brick are 13 inches thick, and each room is 20 by 20 feet with 13 foot ceilings. The doors are pegged, and many have the original locks, which were made in London. Ashlawn has had several prominent owners, including Tennessee ironmaster Montgomery Bell. It was restored to its original splendor by Mr. and Mrs. Stirton Oman.

Inglehame

Inglehame was built in the late 1850's by James Hazard Wilson II for his son James Hazard Wilson III and his wife Virginia Zollicoffer, the daughter of Civil War General Felix Zollicoffer, who was killed at the Battle of Fishing Creek. Inglehame was originally called Harpeth.

Green Pastures

Green Pastures, originally called Hadleywood, was built in 1840 by Denny Porterfield and Elizabeth Smith Hadley. The house was built in the style of an English manor house with bricks made by slaves on the site.

Valley View Farm

Valley View Farm was the home of the late Mary Sneed Jones, descendant of Revolutionary War veteran James Sneed, one of the first settlers in the Brentwood area. The house, built of native woods in 1880, still features the original poplar siding and shutters. The house was built by the Tom Oden heirs and was bought by the Sneed-Jones family in 1901. The original Brentwood post office stands in the yard.

Stone Fences

Stone fences, characteristic of the Brentwood landscape, are widely thought to have been built by slave labor, but probably were constructed by Irish residents.

still standing is on land as of this date owned by Marie Little Ehresman. The original part of that log house was built around 1810. Miriam Fly Hildebrand, an Edmondson descendant, as of the date of this writing lives on Edmondson Pike on land that has been in her family since the 1790's.

"Some of the original Edmondson land is still owned by Edmondson descendants."

The Hill Family

One of the most influential families in the early days of Brentwood was that of Green Hill, who came to Williamson County in 1799 from his home in Louisburg, North Carolina. He named his new home in the wilderness Liberty Hill after his home in North Carolina. Green Hill founded the Liberty Church, and the surrounding community took its name from the church.

Green Hill was the son of Green and Grace Bennett Hill of Tidewater, Virginia, a family of wealth and influence. Early in his life, he dedicated himself to two causes: Colonial independence and Methodism. He was a member of the North Carolina Provincial Congress from the Halifax District. He served as Justice of the Peace, County Court Clerk of Franklin County, and a delegate to the Confederation Congress in 1785.

Green Hill also served as State Treasurer for the Halifax District of North Carolina from 1779 to 1785. He is credited with saving the State Treasury from the advancing Cornwallis army. Holding the rank of Major, Green Hill served with the North Carolina Militia. He later served for twelve months active duty in the North Carolina Continental Army as chaplain.

As a lay preacher, Green Hill was instrumental in the spread of Methodism in North Carolina and Tennessee. His home, Liberty Hill in Louisburg, was the scene of the first Annual Conference of the Methodist Church in America in 1785. Three subsequent conferences were held there: in 1790, 1791, and 1794. It was no doubt a desire to take Methodism to the frontier that motivated Green Hill to move to Middle Tennessee.

Green Hill bought the grant that became Liberty Hill from Randolph Humphries in 1786. Tradition has it that he first came to the Cumberland country in 1796, staying in the safety of Fort Nashboro until his home was completed in 1799.

Green Hill died at his home in the Liberty Community November 3, 1826. In honor of his exemplary life and his work in the Methodist Church, a marker was erected at the Green Hill Cemetery bearing the following inscription:

Green Hill moved from North Carolina to a large plantation of which this is a center in 1799. Hill was a Revolutionary War colonel, a generous philanthropist and a Methodist preacher for over fifty years. On October 17, 1808, he entertained the ninth session of the Western Conference of the Methodist Church at this place. The cemetery near by in which Hill and his family are buried was given by 58 descendants to the Tennessee Conference of the Methodist Church on June 25, 1960, and was accepted as a Methodist Shrine.

In his will, probated in January 1826, Green Hill left 195 acres to his daughter, Lucy Cannon. This land is now Seratoga Hills Subdivision. The balance of his land he left to his son, Joshua Cannon Hill. At his death, Green Hill owned eight slaves, whom he left to his children. In his will, he had the following to say about the institution of slavery:

> Respecting my colored people whom I now possess, it is my sincere desire that whenever Government shall permit that they all be liberated for I consider slavery to be unjust and inconsistent with Spirit and doctrine of the Gospel of Christ. But under present law we are restrained that liberty, therefore until that desirable event shall take place I dispose of them as follows . . .

The original Green Hill house was torn down in the 1920's to make way for a more modern residence. Today all that is left of the original structure on the site is the smoke house.

The Hunt Family

At the intersection of Edmondson Pike and Concord Road are three homes, occupied at the date of this manuscript by members of the Little family on land that had been in their family since 1799. These men are descendants of Gersham Hunt who was one of the first settlers in the Brentwood area.

Gersham Hunt was born in Rowan County, North Carolina, in 1765. In 1799, he purchased the land that became the Hunt homeplace. The original Hunt home was a two-story log structure, which stood just to the rear of the present home of William Robert Little. The old log home burned in 1939.

The father of Gersham Hunt of Williamson County, Tennessee, was Jonathan Hunt. He is buried in the Eaton Cemetery near Cana, North Carolina. Jonathan Hunt was appointed a Justice of the Peace in Rowan County in 1753. He served as a Colonel in the North Carolina Militia, taking an active part in putting down

Indian uprisings. He also commanded a company during the Revolutionary War and was a member of the Safety Commission of Rowan County. He is said to have been the first man to receive General George Washington upon the general's arrival at Salisbury, North Carolina.

Gersham Hunt came to Williamson County in the late 1700's and was prominent in early Williamson County affairs. He was the leader of the militia company from his district, and was a Justice of the Peace. He frequently sat as judge at the General Sessions Court in Franklin and was a farmer and slaveholder as well.

Gersham Hunt died in 1838. His wife, Sarah Orton Hunt, died in 1849. Both are buried in the Hunt cemetery on the old family farm.

After the death of his father, William Carroll Hunt, who was a lawyer practicing in Franklin, continued to live with his mother at the homeplace. He subsequently acquired the interests of his brothers and sisters in the land. He died in 1860, and his widow Elizabeth Ames Ogilvie Hunt conveyed "for love and affection" her dower interest in the land to her three children. That same year the land was partitioned among the three children. The portion of the land still owned by Hunt descendants was partitioned to William Gersham Hunt.

William Gersham Hunt, son of William Carroll Hunt, was a surveyor by trade, and served for many years as the county surveyor of Williamson County. He had two daughters who were the first and second wives of Robert Milton Little. The present owners of the Hunt place are the sons of Robert Milton Little and the Hunt sisters.

The Frost Family

The Frost family came to the Brentwood area from Newberry, South Carolina, around 1810. They bought land on Old Smyrna Road that was described as being a part of the old Mayfield Station tract. They built their home near an old Indian town and at the site of the old Mayfield Station.

"The Frost place, known as Cotton Port, was situated on Old Smyrna Road and was the center of commercial activity."

Captain John Frost and his wife, Rhoda Miles Frost, were the first Frosts in the Brentwood area. They were married in Newberry, South Carolina, where the first of their children was born. The other children were born after they arrived in Tennessee. Shortly after their arrival, they began to build their home, which still stands on Old Smyrna Road and is still in the Frost family. The Frost place, known as Cotton Port, was situated on Old Smyrna Road and soon became the center of commerical activity in the area. The gristmill, the post office, and the community store were located there.

John Frost earned his title as Captain when he became commander of a company during the War of 1812. In 1829, he donated the land on which the Old Smyrna Church was built. This chuch was in existence until 1939 when it was disbanded and merged with the Brentwood Methodist Church.

The Frost family was originally of Quaker persuasion, and their path followed that of the Quaker migration in America. They probably originated in Pennsylvania, but they are first identified in the Hopewell Monthly Meeting Quaker settlement in Frederick County, Virginia, founded in the 1730's.

In the mid 1700's, the Quakers of Hopewell migrated south, settling in North Carolina and South Carolina. The Frosts and the related families of Miles, Hollingsworth, Taylor, O'Neal and others migrated to South Carolina and settled on the Bush River. The area, known as Quaker Meadows, was located in the Union District of South Carolina and became known as the Bush River Meeting.

It is a well known fact that during the Revolutionary War the colonists fought three groups: the British, the Loyalists (known as Tories) and the Indians. It was open and hostile warfare, and, as in most wars, there were no holds barred. All the horrors of war were visited upon the Tories as well as the British and the Indians. The Frost family, who sided with the Tories, was not spared any of these hardships.

Jonathan Frost, the father of Captain John Frost, was killed by Colonial forces while defending a fort on the Tiger River in South Carolina. His widow, Mary Benson Frost, was left with four small children, all under ten years of age. As a result of their loyalist activities, the Frost property was confiscated by the Colonial government after the war, and the family was reduced to poverty. Jonathan Frost did not receive compensation for his service; consequently, in 1782, an appeal was made to the British government by his widow. She was awarded 30 pounds sterling as a result of this appeal.

John Frost and his three sisters grew to adulthood in South Carolina. Each of them married and all migrated to Tennessee and settled in Williamson County, where many of their descendants still reside.

The Herbert Family

The Herbert family lives on land on Old Smyrna Road and Edmondson Pike that has been in their family since the early 1800's. They are descended from John Herbert, an Englishman, who settled in Virginia before the Revolutionary War. Two of his sons, Nathaniel, born in Virginia in 1772, and Richard, born in Virginia in 1777, migrated to and settled in the Brentwood area. This numerous family intermarried with most of the early Brentwood and Williamson County families.

Robert Nathaniel Herbert, Jr., grandson of Richard Herbert, lived at Brentwood as a boy, and enlisted in Company B of the 20th Tennessee Regiment during the War Between the States. This company was formed in the Brentwood area. Long after the war was over, a questionnaire was circulated to veterans to compile information on these veterans and their service. The questionnaire as filled out by Robert Nathaniel Herbert in 1922 when he was 79 years old reveals some interesting insights into the Herbert family and their life prior to the war.

In the questionnaire, Herbert revealed that his family owned 14 slaves and 300 acres of land at the time of the war. He valued the land at 50 dollars an acre and the slaves at 18 thousand dollars. He stated that the family lived in a six room log and frame house with four plastered rooms. In response to a question asking what kind of work he did as a young man, he replied: "When school was out, I plowed with the Negroes until crops were laid by and all other work to be done finished. Every neighbor was a slave owner. Their boys worked on the farms with the slaves."

In response to a question about what kind of work his parents did, he stated: "My father managed his farm, put handles on plows, made gates for the farm. My mother looked after all work done in the house with two Negro women to do the cooking, spinning and weaving, and making clothes for all the family. The Negroes wore the best of cotton and jeans clothes all made at home and I wore the same. Servants were well fed."

"Herbert revealed that his family owned 14 slaves and 300 acres of land at the time of the Civil War."

When questioned about his schooling, he said that he attended local "subscription" schools for eight years. These were private schools with terms six to seven months long, and mostly male faculty members.

Robert Nathaniel Herbert stated than he enlisted in the army on May 17, 1861, and trained for six months at Camp Trousdale, Tennessee. His first battle was a skirmish at Rockcastle in East Tennessee and he was later in the Battle of Fishing Creek, where General Felix Zollicoffer was killed. He also fought in the Battles of Shiloh, Greenville, and Bull's Gap, and was discharged at Washington, Georgia.

After the war, Herbert stated that he entered the Medical Department of the University of Nashville where he graduated in March, 1867. When he completed the survey, he had been practicing medicine for over 50 years.

The Oden Family

The Odens were another early Brentwood family. The progenitor was one Solomon Oden, born in Maryland and came to Tennessee around 1815. They lived in the southern part of Williamson County before buying land on the Franklin Pike at the corner of Old Smyrna Road. A son, Solomon Fletcher Oden, was long a part of the Brentwood community.

Dr. Oden was born in 1848 and received his medical training at the University of

Nashville. He practiced medicine in Brentwood for over 50 years and married his first cousin, Mary Sophronia Oden. She died in 1934, and he in 1942.

In addition to his general practice, Dr. Oden served as company doctor for the railroad when the huge cut was made in Brentwood in the early 1900's and when Radnor Yards were built. His ledgers for 1887 show that he made day visits for $1.50 and night visits for $2.00. His fee for delivering a baby was $10.00.

The Oden's daughter, Rebecca, married Charles Howell, and they lived for many years at the Direct Oil (now Trammell Crow) site. Their grandson, Charles A. Howell, III, at this writing is serving as Commissioner of Conservation for the State of Tennessee.

The Moore Family

For his services in the Revolutionary War, General Robert Irvin in 1790 received a 640-acre grant "on the waters at the Little Harpeth River" bounded by James Crockett, James Leiper, Christopher Funkhouser, and Thomas Evans. He deeded this grant to his daughter, Eleanor, and her husband, James Moore. They sold 320 acres of the land to Robert Caruthers and made their way from North Carolina in the 1790's to settle on the land.

Eleanor Irvin Moore died in 1809 of typhoid fever and is buried at the Liberty Methodist Church, just off Concord Road. James Moore later married Sarah Alfred, of a family who lived where Hearthstone Subdivision now stands.

James Moore's first home was a two-story log house on Wilson Pike about a mile south of the current Brentwood town center. It was the first house in the area to have glass windows that could be raised and lowered. Its tall chimneys were damaged by the earthquake of 1811, the same quake that formed Reelfoot Lake. The chimneys had to be rebuilt.

"The altered plans of Mooreland are said to be the reason for the off-centered door."

James Moore died in 1838, and his son Robert Irvin Moore became the builder of Mooreland, which is located on Franklin Road in the Koger Center. Another son, Alexander, lived on Moore's Lane and gave his name to that road. Robert Irvin Moore began construction of Mooreland in 1846 and died two years later. The unfinished house was completed under the supervision of Alexander Moore, who revised the plans and built a less commodious house than his brother had originally planned. The altered plans are said to be the reason for the off-center door. The original plans had called for a centered door, and for as large a wing on the left as was completed on the right side of the door.

70

The completed house contains 28 rooms, with a full basement where the house servants lived. The woodwork is bird's-eye maple, and a part of the metal roof came from England. Its Greek Revival architectural style is typical of fine country homes of the period. It was designed for gracious living, with wide halls, large rooms, and 14-foot ceilings. The 15-foot entrance hall, with a winding three-story staircase, is flanked by double parlors, four bedrooms, the nursery, and the dining room, along with connecting hallways. From the L-shaped back porch, a "dog trot" leads to the kitchen where meals were prepared until 1944.

Robert Irvin Moore's son, Hugh Campbell Moore, was to become the owner and longtime resident of Mooreland. He was in his early teens when the War Between the States began, and at age 14 ran away from home to join the Confederate forces. The authorities refused to enlist him, but did agree to keep him as a water boy when he refused to return home to his mother.

During the war, Mooreland was used by both Confederate and Union armies. After the Battle of Nashville, it was used as a hospital. A beautiful grove of ash trees surrounding the house is said to have been cut down by Union soldiers.

After the war, Hugh Campbell returned to Mooreland and later married Kate Jones Greer. They and their three sons lived at Mooreland for many years. All three sons were accomplished musicians, and none of them ever married. One of the sons, Robert Irvin Moore IV, was the organist at Brentwood Methodist Church for over 20 years. After the death of their parents and their brother Hugh Campbell Moore, Jr., Robert and his brother Allen sold Mooreland in 1944. After Mooreland left the Moore family, it was the home of Mr. and Mrs. Oscar Noel and Mr. and Mrs. Albert Maloney.

No story of Mooreland would be complete without reference to Ruth, the daughter of Robert Irvin Moore. On the eve of her wedding, she was found dead in her upstairs room. There has never been an explanation for her mysterious death. Later, residents contend that the ghost of Ruth still inhabits Mooreland. Thus, perhaps the structure still remains in Moore hands, even though at the publication of this work it is the headquarters for the Koger Company and is the center of its low-density office complex.

The McGavock Family

Midway, located on the site of the Brentwood Country Club, was originally a 640 acre grant to James Crockett of Wythe County, Virginia. The land passed into the hands of his daughter, Emily, who married Lysander McGavock, son of David McGavock, early Nashville settler and Register of the Land Office of Tennessee until 1838. The first home built by Emily and Lysander McGavock burned in 1840 and they immediately built the present structure. By his death in 1855, Lysander McGavock had increased his holdings to 1,269 acres.

From 1855 until late in the 1800's Midway was owned by the four daughters of

Emily and Lysander McGavock. Their two sons died when they were in their teens. Emily, who married Oliver Bliss Hayes, Jr., was the only daughter who had children. In turn Midway was divided between their two children Margaret Hayes Powell and Lysander McGavock Hayes. It is still owned by the children of these two.

Midway saw much activity during the Civil War. Soldiers from both armies were frequently on the grounds. A McGavock descendant tells of her grandfather, McGavock Hayes, being "kidnapped" when he was a child by Confederate soldiers. They were scouting in the area and had been seen by the child; consequently, they were afraid that he would tell passing Yankees of their presence. He was returned to the family that night with appropriate explanation.

Family tradition has it that the house was probably saved from being burned by Cynthia McGavock, one of the four sisters who met the Yankees at the door and pled with them not to burn the house.

"Midway was occupied by five generations of McGavocks. It was leased in 1954 to the Brentwood Country Club."

Midway was occupied by five generations of McGavocks. It was leased in 1954 to the Brentwood Country Club. When the golf course was built, well preserved trenches and breastworks were found. Many Indian artifacts have also been found on the grounds at Midway.

Boxwood Hall, situated in what is now Meadow Lake Subdivision, was built in 1852 by Emily McGavock Hayes and her husband, Oliver Bliss Hayes, Jr., on land given to her by her father, Lysander McGavock, builder of Midway. The original house burned while the couple was on their honeymoon, and another slightly smaller house was built. This house, referred to as "the cottage," was incorporated into the present structure.

The lumber in the original part of the house came from trees cut on the property. The bricks were also made there.

A succession of owners has enlarged the house from its original size. The A. J. Dyers bought the property in 1935 and added to the house and built an eight acre lake fed by several springs on the place. A stone spring house where food was stored before the days of refrigeration is located at one of the springs. At one time the lake furnished water for Brentwood's first two subdivisions, Meadow Lake and Iroquois, which were developed on land that originally went with the house. Elizabeth Hayes, daughter of Oliver Bliss and Emily McGavock Hayes, married Dr. W. W. Martin, a Methodist minister and Professor of Hebrew at Vanderbilt University. In the early 1900's they built the present house of hand-cut stone from a private quarry located where the Brentwood Baptist Church now stands.

The front room on the main floor opens across the full width of the house with fireplaces at either end. There are ten fireplaces in the house. The second floor includes six bedrooms and a study. On the third floor there are six more bedrooms.

Boxwood Hall was bought in 1965 by Nell and Jim Fowler, who have dedicated themselves to restoring the mansion to its original magnificence.

The land around Boxwood Hall has yielded many artifacts of the past. A major archaeological dig was conducted there because of its being a site where Indians lived. Also, many Civil War artifacts have been found, attesting to military activity in the area.

Green Pastures

Green Pastures, located on Franklin Road, is certainly one of Brentwood's finest homes. The house was built in the style of an English manor house, with bricks made by slaves on the site. Its ivy-covered walls rise to a commanding view of the grounds that gives it an appearance of an English country estate. The woodwork is hand-carved, and the floors are white oak.

Green Pastures was built in 1840 and called Hadleywood at that time. It was built by Denny Porterfield Hadley and his wife Elizabeth Smith Hadley. Mrs. Hadley was the daughter of Sarah Jane Leiper, who married Alexander Smith. It will be remembered that Sarah Jane Leiper was the daughter of early Nashville settler James Leiper, who was killed in an Indian raid at Fort Nashboro a few months after his wedding and before the birth of his daughter. A 640-acre grant was awarded to his heirs posthumously. This grant was located in Brentwood and was taken up by Sarah Jane Leiper and her husband Alexander Smith. The land on which Green Pastures was built was a gift to Elizabeth Smith Hadley by her mother Sarah Jane Leiper Smith.

Elizabeth Smith's husband Denny Porterfield Hadley was the son of early Williamson County settler Joshua Hadley, who was a captain in the First North Carolina Infantry during the Revolutionary War. He fought in several battles and was wounded at the Battle of King's Mountain. Joshua Hadley had the distinction of being one of the original members of the Society of Cincinnati, a prestigious organization made up of first sons of Revolutionary patriots. Both Elizabeth Smith Hadley and Denny Porterfield Hadley are buried in the Hadley Cemetery on Concord Road.

"Union and Confederate forces alike camped on the grounds of Green Pastures."

Union and Confederate forces alike camped on the grounds of Green Pastures during the War Between the States. Confederate General Nathan Bedford Forrest's troop camped there. After the Battle of Nashville, the house was commandeered as a hospital by Union troops. One soldier was ordered to be shot for using abusive language toward Mrs. Hadley, who had several sons in the Confederate Army.

In its heyday, Green Pastures boasted fine gardens, grounds and orchards. The wrought iron gate at the garden was said to have come from Killarney Castle, and a sun dial in the garden reportedly belonged to Anne Boleyn, ill-fated wife of Henry VIII.

Mountview

It is hard to believe that Mountview, situated on Franklin Road, was completed and sold by its builder within four years of its completion. The builder was William P. Davis, long-time Brentwood resident. His wife was Judith Robertson Owen, the daughter of Everett Owen, who lived in a fine brick house nearby. Mountview was begun and completed in troubled times: it was finished in 1861 after the War Between the States had begun, and was sold shortly after the war was over.

Mountview's style is starkly Greek Revival, with tall trim columns heavily moulded along the roof line. On the interior, the wide entrance hall is flanked by large parlors and a circular staircase. The baseboards are deep, and the ceilings are eleven feet high with handsome mouldings and deep door frames.

"While spending the evening at Mountview, Ashley B. Rozell, a Methodist minister, bought the place."

In the fall of 1865, a lone horseman rode up to the door of Mountview and asked for lodging for the evening. The stranger was Ashley B. Rozell, a Methodist minister, large land owner, and successful businessman. He was on his way to Franklin to buy an estate there. During the course of the evening, he changed his mind and bought Mountview instead. Thus, the Rozell family became Brentwood residents, and remained so for over 60 years. They were prominent people, and active in local affairs.

Ashley Rozell, who was of French Huguenot descent, was ordained as a Methodist minister in 1822 and served various churches in the Tennessee Conference until he retired from the ministry in 1833. His father Solomon Rozell was a pioneer in West Tennessee and Memphis and became a wealthy landowner there.

Although Ashley B. Rozell had retired from the ministry, he never lost his interest either in religion or in the Methodist Church. He was instrumental in the founding of the Brentwood United Methodist Church, and contributed generously to the building fund of its structure on Church Street that was completed in 1886. Reports are that the church at one time was named for Ashley B. Rozell.

Ashley Rozell died in 1886, a man of considerable wealth. He owned 1,640 acres in Arkansas, several lots in Memphis and a large tract in Texas in addition to his

Brentwood holdings. Mountview remained in the Rozell family until it was sold to Charles P. Wilson in 1925.

The Wilsons made improvements for the sake of convenience, installing baths and building a screened porch to connect the house with the detached kitchen. They also added a back staircase so that the upstairs traffic would not be limited to the front winding staircase.

Mr. Wilson was for a long time Magistrate to the Quarterly Court of Williamson County. His heirs sold the property to Ray Bell in 1980.

Ashlawn

Like its neighbor Green Pastures, Ashlawn was built on Franklin Road on the James Leiper grant by one of the children of Sarah Jane Leiper Smith. That builder was Mary Emeline Smith and her husband Richard Christmas. They were deeded 200 acres of the Leiper grant by Sarah Jane Leiper Smith and her husband Alexander Smith.

Little is known of Richard Christmas other than the fact that he was a person of great wealth and impeccable taste. There are legends of his great coach drawn by six matching horses, of his fine clothes and urbane manners. His main residence was a Mississippi plantation, and Ashlawn served only as a summer home.

"Ashlawn was built with meticulous attention to detail."

Ashlawn was built with meticulous attention to detail. Walls of handmade brick are 13 inches thick and all rooms are 20×20 with 13 foot ceilings. The stone veranda, columns, and mantels are from limestone quarried on location, as is a cellar lined with limestone. Doors are pegged and many have the original hardware. The woodwork is yellow poplar except for the downstairs hall floor, which is white ash. Both the handrail and spindles of the staircase are made of cherry. In the entrance hall is a curved wall and winding staircase that rises to the third floor.

There were but two children born to Mary Emeline and Richard Christmas. One son, Richard Jr., died when he was 14 months old. The other son lived to manhood, but mysteriously disappeared while on a trip and was never heard from again. Mrs. Christmas herself died in 1842 at the age of 27 as a result of a steamboat accident on the Mississippi River.

In 1839, Richard Christmas sold Ashlawn. It passed through a number of hands until 1851 when it was purchased by Montgomery Bell, wealthy ironmaster of Dickson County. While in his hands the house was greatly abused by careless and indifferent servants. Bell was a bachelor, and apparently cared little for the amenities of home life.

It was not until 1871 that Ashlawn again became the center of family life. At that time it was bought by Henry Zellner of Maury County. He had two daughters, both of whom married men who lived in the Brentwood area. Margaret Ophelia married David Lipscomb, teacher at Lipscomb School on Concord Road and founder of David Lipscomb College. Another daughter, Mary Jane, married William Callender and lived at the railroad crossing on Concord Road.

Henry Zellner died in 1879, and the farm passed to his son, James Jr. For a number of years, his daughter Lucy taught a private school for neighboring children in the old brick office. James Zellner died in 1905, and Ashlawn was sold to Andrew Mizell, well-known Nashville wholesale grocer, and his wife, Lucy Merrill Mizell. The Mizell family lived at Ashlawn for 37 years.

In 1945, Ashlawn was bought by Mr. and Mrs. Stirton Oman. They remodeled the house extensively. The one-story columns which had been at the front of the house were moved to the side door, and two-story columns were erected at the front as well as across the back. The old kitchen and office were joined to the side of the house, and other changes were made both inside and out. As of this writing, Ashlawn remains the home of Mrs. Stirton Oman.

The Wilson Family

The progenitor of the Wilson family was James Hazard Wilson. Born in 1763 in County Fermanaugh, Ireland, he came to America and settled in North Carolina, where he married Ruth Davidson. They had nine children, all of whom married into the most influential families in the South and became prominent in their own right. One of these children was James Hazard Wilson II, who settled in Williamson County and for whom Wilson Pike was named.

In addition to his vast Wilson Pike plantation, James Hazard Wilson had extensive holdings in other southern states as well. He owned sugar plantations in Louisiana and operated a steamboat line on the Mississippi River. He was also instrumental in building a suspension bridge in Nashville. It is said that he transported his slaves from the Deep South to Tennessee during the summer to a more healthy and comfortable climate.

James Hazard Wilson II married his cousin Emeline in 1821. She was the daughter of Samuel D. Wilson, who became one of the first Secretaries of State in Texas. Best man at the wedding was Sam Houston, who became Texas' first governor. Wilson was a staunch supporter of the Confederacy during the Civil War. He is said to have spent $10,000 outfitting an entire company during the conflict.

Ravenswood

Ravenswood, on Wilson Pike, was completed in 1825 by James Hazard Wilson

II. It was named for his friend Sam Houston. The home is of classic Federal design, rising from hand-hewn limestone foundation blocks. A large entrance hall is flanked with parlors, each with a fireplace. The original springhouse, built of limestone and covered with ivy, is still in use. Two of the original 13 slave cabins, as well as the kitchen, have been restored. Today the house, the brick kitchen, and row of brick slave houses are in a beautiful state of preservation. It is owned by Mr. and Mrs. Reece Smith.

Inglehame

Inglehame, located at Wilson Pike and Split Log Road, was built in the late 1850's by James Hazard Wilson II for his son, James Hazard Wilson III and his wife, Virginia Zollicoffer, daughter of Confederate General Felix Zollicoffer. The family resided on the corner of Sixth Avenue and Demonbreun Street in Nashville, the building that for many years was the home of the Elks' Club. General Zollicoffer was killed at the Battle of Fishing Creek, and thus was the first Confederate General killed in the Civil War. After his death, Virginia Zollicoffer Wilson was returning home from Nashville along Wilson Pike when her carriage was stopped by Union troops under the command of General William Nelson. When her identity and the fact that she was in mourning for her father were discovered, General Nelson ordered his troops to let the carriage pass while they stood in silent respect for the daughter of the slain Confederate general.

Inglehame was originally called Harpeth because the spring is located on the property that gives rise to the Little Harpeth River. It featured imported marble mantels and finely carved woodwork. The old brick kitchen is still in the yard, and the log smokehouse was reconstructed from materials found in cabins on the place. James Hazard Wilson III sold this house in 1877 to Major John E. Tulloss. It remained in that family until 1938 when it was bought by Mr. and Mrs. Vernon Sharp. They conducted extensive remodeling and restoration work. Just as the house was nearing completion, it was gutted by fire. The Sharps again rebuilt the house using the exterior walls which were left intact.

"Inglehame was originally called Harpeth because the spring located on the property gives rise to the Little Harpeth River."

Century Oak

Century Oak, on Wilson Pike, was built in the 1840's by James Hazard Wilson II for his son, Samuel Wilson and his wife, Lucy Ann Marshall. The house was originally a three story structure with twin chimneys tied together with parapet walls extending over the roof. The present hip roof was added in the 1920's when the original roof was blown away in a storm. The house features a circular staircase that winds to the third floor ballroom. It is said that the Wilsons blindfolded their horses during the Civil War and led them to the ballroom to hide them from raiding Federals. Eight of the original twelve fireplaces are still in use. Carved arches framed by Ionic panels connect the parlors. The walls are twelve inches thick and the ceilings are twelve feet eight inches high. The original two story brick kitchen can still be seen in the yard.

"Horses were blindfolded and led into the ballroom of Century Oak to save them from the Federals."

The house was originally surrounded by giant oaks. It is said that over 20 of these oak trees were cut when the railroad was built in front of the house in 1912.

Century Oak remained in the hands of the Wilson family until 1927. During the 1940's it was owned by Edward Potter, founder of Nashville's Commerce Union Bank. At this writing it is owned by Mrs. Sam M. Stubblefield.

Isola Bella

Isola Bella, situated on Franklin Road, was built around 1840 by James and Narcissa Merritt Johnston. The property originally belonged to David Johnston, one of the first settlers on the Cumberland and grandfather of the builder. During the Civil War, the lawn of Isola Bella was traversed by both Confederate and Federal cannons, wagons, and marching soldiers. It served as a meeting place for General John Bell Hood and his staff before the Battle of Nashville, and as a hospital for the wounded and dying after that ill fated battle. When the house was no longer owned by the Johnston family, it stood vacant for many years and fell into a serious state of disrepair.

"Isola Bella served as a hospital after the Battle of Nashville."

The house was bought in the 1940's and restored by Mr. and Mrs. John Oman. They named it Thurso after the Oman ancestral home in Scotland. After Mrs. Oman's death, it was bought by Mr. and Mrs. Dave Alexander, who undertook extensive remodeling and landscaping. They named the house Isola Bella.

Old pictures show that Isola Bella originally had a one-story veranda with bannisters on the ground level and around the porch roof, which was supported by eight slender columns. It did not have the pediments and tall pillars which distinguish the north and west today.

The Owen Family

The Owen family was in the Brentwood area at an early date and built several fine homes. The Owen-Primm House on Moores Lane was built by Jabez Owen, a prominent early Brentwood physician. It was built in the classic simplicity of a Middle Tennessee plantation house with four columns supporting the two story porch. The slave cabins are still intact along the drive leading to the rear of the house. The original log house is incorporated into the present house, and one log bears the date of 1806. Today the house is owned by the Primm family, a family of equally deep roots in the Brentwood community.

Maple Lawn, also on Moores Lane, was built by Nathan and Jane Hightower Owen in the 1830's on a three hundred acre tract of land that was an original land grant to John Cockrill. The property was sold in 1876 to N. N. Cox of Hickman County, who started out as a poor boy but worked and educated himself as a lawyer and soon proved to be a criminal lawyer without match in this section. During the Civil War, he was a colonel of the 10th Tennessee Cavalry and was twice commended for bravery by Forrest. Maple Lawn was remodeled in the 1870's, giving it the present Victorian look. The square columns at the front were replaced by Ionic columns and the bay window was added at that time.

Clover Lawn, on Wilson Pike, was another Owen home. It was located on the plantation which is now Brentmeade Estates and was identical to Maple Lawn. Both homes were remodeled in the late 1800's, at which time the bay windows and metal Ionic columns were added. Both homes had three columns.

Clover Lawn was built in the 1850's by Robert Rowland Owen. It had 18-inch-thick brick walls, and the staircase and woodwork were of exceptionally fine quality. Unfortunately, Clover Lawn was structurally unsound either because of a poor foundation or an inferior quality of bricks. It was rebuilt later after iron rods were inserted into the structure to stabilize it. Clover Lawn was purchased by Frank Gasser, a native of Switzerland, in 1927. It remained in that family until 1985, when the developer of Brentmeade demolished the house. The Gasser heirs saved the hand-carved staircase.

The Crockett Family

The Crockett family was in the Brentwood area at an early date. James Crockett received a 640-acre land grant which included what is now the Brentwood Country Club. His daughter married a McGavock, and the land passed into the McGavock family.

The Knox Crockett house on Wilson Pike was built by Major Andrew Crockett, who settled here in 1799. At that time, Major Crockett had to take his rifle with him to the back fields to protect the workers from Indian attack. Typical of early architecture, the house was originally two log rooms with a "dog trot." Later, a second story was added. The logs were covered with clapboards, and the out-buildings were joined to the main structure. The kitchen was a separate building in the back. A skirmish occurred on the grounds of the Knox Crockett house during the Civil War, and the family still has many of the artifacts that remained after the skirmish.

Forge Seat was built in 1808 by Samuel Crockett on a 640-acre Revolutionary War Grant to his father, Andrew Crockett. It is built of brick laid in Flemish bond and the interior resembles Independence Hall in Philadelphia. Built before the central hall came into vogue, each room has a staircase that goes to the room above. The floors are random width white ash. The Crocketts operated an iron forge on this site. Andrew Jackson stopped at Forge Seat on his way to New Orleans during the War of 1812 to purchase arms for his men. A few of the Crockett rifles are still in existence and may be identified by S&AC engraved on the barrel. Ownership of Forge Seat passed from the Crockett family to the Jabez Owen family, who established their cemetery next to the Crockett Cemetery across the road from the house. Later owners, the Carpenters, ran a store, which can still be seen in the yard.

Crockett Springs, on Moore's Lane, was built by Joseph Crockett who came to the Brentwood area in 1808 to take up the 640 acres willed to him by his father, John Crockett, who died in 1799 in Wythe County, Virginia. Joseph Crockett married his first cousin, Polly Crockett, and they reared a large family. The house, built of logs cut on the place, originally fronted the old road that ran from Wilson Pike to Nashville Pike, the bed of which can still be plainly seen between the house and the cemetery. The stone chimney in the kitchen is original, and the outline of the old house can be seen under the framing. It remained in the family until 1955. The house was restored by Glenn Noble, and today forms the central part of the clubhouse for Crockett Springs National Golf and Country Club.

The Sneed Family

The Sneed family roots in America extend to Colonial times, when William Sneed, his wife, Joan, and their son, William, located in James County, Virginia, in 1635 when the first generation of English settlers migrated to America. The ancestral home of the Sneeds still stands in Keele, Staffordshire, England. Its grounds are now a modern university, but the old manor house remains on its original site, and the Sneed coat-of-arms is permanently emblazoned above the mantle in the great hall.

In true pioneer spirit, James Sneed and his wife Bethenia Harden Perkins Sneed brought their family to the Brentwood area in 1798. In so doing, they were one of the first families to arrive in the area at a time when settlers were still being ravaged by Indian attacks. Most of the settlers in the Brentwood area sought shelter in Mayfields Fort, but James Sneed built a one-room log cabin a few hundred yards from Mayfields Fort. This cabin still stands, and is incorporated into the larger home of Mr. and Mrs. G. W. Renegar and Miss Callie Lillie Owen on Old Smyrna Road.

James Sneed, son of Zachariah Sneed and Martha (Patsy) Nance Sneed, came to Brentwood from Virginia. He and his wife raised 12 children, three of whom built substantial homes on Old Smyrna Road and all of whom married into prominent families. The name "Sneed" came to be synonymous with civic and religious leadership in the community.

The Sneeds were extensively interrelated with other prominent early families in the Middle Tennessee area. James Sneed's brother William Sneed and his wife Mary DeLoach Sneed settled in the area as well in what is now Chickering Estates. Bethenia Sneed's uncle, Thomas Harden Perkins, also made the treacherous journey from Virginia to Tennessee, and eventually built a substantial home west of Franklin. This house was called "Meeting of the Waters," and still stands in its original splendor. Bethenia Perkins' brother, Nicholas Tate Perkins, built Poplar Grove, a prominent Williamson County residence. Bethenia's cousin Nicholas Perkins distinguished himself not only by constructing Montpier but also by capturing Aaron Burr and delivering him to Federal authorities in Washington. Yet another family member was William Giles Harding, who built Belle Meade Mansion.

Sneed Acres is the original log cabin built on Old Smyrna Road by James Sneed. The stone chimneys use the stepback method of construction. Four log rooms divided by a hall have been covered by weather boarding. The dining room and kitchen are separated from the house by a dog trot. Present occupants of the house are Callie Lillie Owen and Mary Sue Owen Renegar, descendants of the builder.

"James Sneed and his wife brought their family to the Brentwood area from Virginia in 1798."

The eldest son of James and Bethenia Perkins Sneed was Constantine Perkins Sneed, born in 1790. He served with General Andrew Jackson in the Indian Wars and in the War of 1812. He returned from the Battle of New Orleans to establish himself on a part of his father's 640-acre grant. In 1825, he married his cousin Susannah Perkins Hardeman. Soon after their marriage, they began to build Windy Hill, which is still visible from Old Smyrna Road.

The walls of Windy Hill rose from a limestone foundation made of bricks molded of clay dug in the front yard. A depression is still visible there. The house was built over a large basement that saw constant use in daily routines in Windy Hill. The basement was never more in use than during the Civil War when Federal troops were foraging in the area. Family heirlooms and other valuables, as well as cattle, were hidden in the basement to keep them from being stolen. It is reported that the women in the family would mount the horses to keep them from being stolen by the Yankees.

During the Civil War, one son of this house, Constantine Perkins Sneed, Jr., a Confederate soldier, received a wound during the Battle of Chickamauga which necessitated the amputation of his leg. He sent word home that he feared the wound would be mortal. Another son, James Hardeman Sneed, also a Confederate soldier, was sent to bring his brother home. The wounded soldier died before he could return home, and his brother buried him in a casket fashioned from planks ripped from the barn.

Another son of this house, Robert Scales Sneed, surveyed the Tennessee-Alabama Railroad charter in 1852, which ran through Brentwood on its way to the Alabama line.

Foxview was built on Old Smyrna Road by Alexander Ewing Sneed, youngest child of pioneer, James Sneed. Two of his sons served in the Confederate Army. Foxview was bought by the Shwab family, who extensively rebuilt and remodeled, using the old house as the central core of the building.

Brentvale was built on Old Smyrna Road in 1830 from huge logs cut on the place by William Temple Sneed, seventh child of pioneer James Sneed. William Temple Sneed was the father of Dr. William J. Sneed, who served as a surgeon during the Civil War. Tradition has it that he met Corporal George Whipple Hubbard, a New England teacher turned medieval corpsman, on the battlefield after the Battle of Franklin. They began to discuss the need for training negroes in medicine. This brief and casual conversation led ultimately to the establishment of Meharry Medical College and Hubbard Hospital. Dr. Sneed became a teacher at Meharry, and was a strong supporter of that institution.

Valley View Farm was the lifelong home of the late Mary Sneed Jones, descendant of Revolutionary War Veteran James Sneed, one of the first settlers in the Brentwood area. This land adjoins the original Sneed grant. The house, built of native woods in 1880, still features the original poplar siding and shutters. The Tom Oden heirs built the house and it was bought by the Sneed-Jones family in 1901. The original Brentwood post office stands in the yard. The first tall house on Wilson Pike (then called Harpeth Turnpike) was across the road from the Sneed house, and they were spaced at two mile intervals along the road.

McCrory House

Brentwood's oldest house is on the Davidson County side of Old Hickory Boulevard, just west of Granny White Pike. Built by Thomas McCrory in 1797, it is said to be the third oldest house still standing in Davidson County.

It was used as a benchmark to describe the boundaries of Williamson County when it was formed out of Davidson in 1799. The description states that the line begins at a point "forty poles due north of the dwelling place of Thomas McCrory." The McCrory house has been beautifully restored, and is currently the home of Raymond White.

The Holt Family

The Holt family came to Brentwood in the early 1800's and settled on what is now Crockett Road. The first members of the Holt family to come to Williamson County were John Holt and his wife Isabella Hardeman Holt. They built a log home on the property where they raised 12 children. One of those children, Thomas Holt, who married Judith Herbert, became the master of the Holt Plantation and added land to it until he owned about 1500 acres.

Wildwood, the home of the Holt family, was built in the 1840's by Thomas and Judith Herbert Holt. Nearby trees provided wood for its construction, and family slaves manufactured bricks on site. The doors are solid walnut with blinds of the same material. The house is three stories high, with tall columns. High-ceiling twin parlors on either side of the wide front hall can be opened by means of massive folding doors so that the front hall becomes a huge ballroom.

In addition to their Brentwood holdings, the Holts had sugar plantations in Louisiana. When Wildwood was built, many of its furnishings were brought up the Mississippi River from New Orleans. Wildwood was one of the largest plantations in the Brentwood area: over 100 slaves were employed there at the time of the Civil War. It had its own cotton gin, saw mill, and grist mill. Many of the slave cabins may still be seen in the "quarters." The blacks had their own church and school on the plantation. The church is still in existence and is known as Edmondson Chapel.

After Thomas Holt's death, his son Lewis Holt inherited Wildwood and the Holt Plantation. He married Elmira Page, and their children became the objects of much attention in the Brentwood community. John Page Holt, who died in 1985, built a small house on the premises when the "big house" became too much of a burden for him and his wife, O'dell. Will Holt lived on the farm across Crockett Road which is now Indian Point Subdivision. The three Holt sisters, Margaret, Rose, and Kate, were gracious hostesses and shared their home with Brentwood residents for years. The perennial social event of the year at Wildwood was the annual Halloween party for the Sunday School of the Brentwood Methodist Church.

In the attic of Wildwood there were several trunks of clothes dating back to the early 1800's. These clothes were borrowed for years by Brentwood residents for parties and plays. The clothes were given to the Carnton Association in Franklin a few years ago.

At this writing, Wildwood is owned by Charles Witherspoon, Jr., whose mother was Kate Holt Witherspoon. He has served for many years as organist of the Brentwood United Methodist Church.

Points of Interest

1. Mooreland
2. Midway/Brentwood Country Club
3. Green Pastures
4. Mountview
5. Ashlawn
6. Owen's Chapel Church of Christ
7. Isola Bella
8. Maple Lawn
9. Crockett Springs
10. Owen-Primm House
11. Boiling Springs Mounds
12. Boiling Springs Academy
13. Century Oak
14. Inglehame
15. Ravenswood
16. Forge Seat
17. Knox-Crockett House
18. Clover Lawn
19. The Hightower Place
20. Cotton Port
21. Brentvale Farm
22. Sneed Acres
23. Windy Hill
24. Foxview
25. Valley View Farm
26. Mayfield
27. The Moore Cabin Site

Brentwood

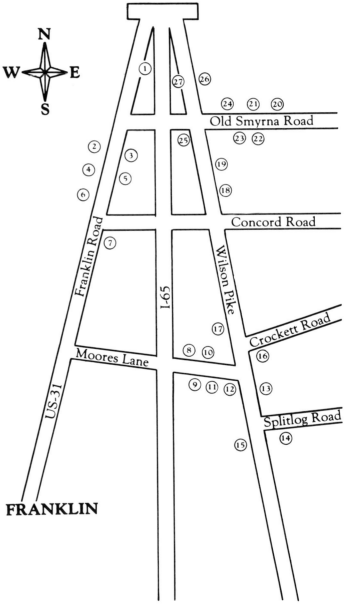

6
Civil War Brentwood

When war clouds began to gather over the South in 1860, Tennessee was undecided as to which way it would cast its lot. Sentiment varied from pro-Union sympathizers in East Tennessee to the equally strong pro-Confederacy sympathizers in West Tennessee. Middle Tennessee fell somewhere in between, not only geographically but in its sentiment. Lincoln's call for troops was enough to push the state squarely into the Confederate camp, and Tennessee became the 11th Confederate State of America.

Last and First

Tennessee was the last to leave the Union and the first to re-enter. Middle Tennessee was the bridge between two extremes of sentiment within the state. Thus, Tennessee, as a border state, became the battleground of the Civil War in the West, and Middle Tennessee saw more than its share of military activity.

Middle Tennessee was a prize that Federal troops took early in the war, consequently driving a wedge into the heart of the Confederacy. The gateways to that heart were the Tennessee and Cumberland Rivers. Two hastily-erected forts, Fort Donelson on the Cumberland and Fort Henry on the Tennessee, fell early in the war, leaving Nashville wide open to Union attack. It fell without a shot in February 1862, and remained firmly in Federal hands until the end of the war, withstanding General John Bell Hood's vain attempt to retake Nashville some two years later. This attempt culminated the Battle of Nashville on December 15 and 16, 1864. Hood's decisive defeat sounded the death knell of the Confederacy.

While Unionist military governor Andrew Johnson ruled from Nashville, the opposing armies clashed at nearby Lebanon, Gallatin, Hartsville, Nolensville, and Thompson Station, with major battles at Shiloh, Murfreesboro (Stones River), and Franklin. Battle lines were indistinct, and areas shifted from being occupied by the Federals to the Confederacy.

Havens for Armies

The rich plantations of Williamson County were sought-after by both sides. Two armies had to be fed and armed, and few plantations were spared their foraging activities. Almost without exception, these plantations were havens for Confederates when they could make their way through Union lines. Provisions and supplies were freely shared. By contrast, the Federals provided for themselves by force. Stories still abound in Brentwood families about the times that the "Yankees came."

The Holts at Wildview on Crockett Road dug up their kitchen floor and hid hams there. The Hunts on Edmondson Pike lost all their horses, but other families devised ingenious solutions to prevent similar occurrences. The Sneeds on Old Smyrna Road hid their horses in the basement of Windy Hill. Despite threats, Mrs. Herbert on Wilson Pike refused to dismount and surrender her horse to Federal troops. The Wilsons at Century Oak on Wilson Pike blindfolded their horses and led them to the third-floor ballroom in the house. Bee hives were overturned at the Roberts home on Wilson Pike, and the bees chased the Yankees away. Dr. William J. McMurray, Brentwood resident and author of a history of the 20th Tennessee Regiment, perhaps said it best: ". . . and a portion of them camped around my mother's house that night; the next morning, not a chicken, turkey, goose, hog, horse, or cow could be found on the place, and not a rail near the house." It was one of those foraging expeditions that led to Forrest's raid on Brentwood.

Nathan Bedford Forrest

Nathan Bedford Forrest was a man of many seasons. Born in poverty near Chapel Hill, Tennessee, he was a millionaire slave trader by the time he enlisted in the Confederate Army at the age of 41. He had only one year of formal education and was almost illiterate. He once said, "I never pick up a pen but what I think of a snake." But most of all, Nathan Bedford Forrest was a military genius. He frequently clashed with his West Point educated fellow officers, but his success where they failed is proof that his instinct was superior to their formal training.

Forrest's potential was recognized by General Beauregard during the Battle of Shiloh, the first major battle on the Western Front. After that battle, Beauregard made Forrest a brigadier general and commissioned him to go forth and harass the enemy in Middle Tennessee. Forrest fulfilled his mission far beyond anyone's highest expectations.

Forrest's raids were quickly executed in places least expected. His men

3D 58
FORREST'S BRENTWOOD RAID

With two brigades of Cavalry in a widely separated encircling or "Pincer" maneuver on the night of March 24, 1863, Brig. Gen. Nathan Bedford Forrest raided deep behind Federal lines. He completely captured the Federal garrison of 785 officers and men with all valuable stores with loss of but one killed and two wounded.

TENNESSEE HISTORICAL COMMISSION

Nathan Bedford Forrest figured prominently in Brentwood's role in the Civil War.

captured thousands of Yankees and tons of supplies. Bridges were removed, roads were blocked, and telegraph lines were torn down. He liberated Murfreesboro and came near enough to Nashville to make military governor Johnson uneasy.

In March 1863, the Union command at Franklin sent out troops and 80 wagons which they hoped to fill with forage from local plantations. Confederate forces met them at Thompson Station, four miles south of Franklin. A battle ensued and Federal forces were routed. They retreated to Franklin and later to Brentwood where they set up camp. One contingency camped at the railroad bridge over the Little Harpeth River, now a pasture owned by the Oman and Henley families. The other contingency camped at what is now Brentwood's town center. Five hundred Wisconsin troops entrenched themselves in a stockade surrounded by "a quarter mile belt of felled trees." Forrest first surrounded the stockade at town center and demanded surrender. The Federal commander replied, "Come and get us." After a single shot, the Federals realized they were surrounded, and promptly surrendered. Forrest then moved on to take the fortification on the Little Harpeth River. His bounty consisted of 800 men and new issues of rifles and ammunition.

Forrest's raid was the last fighting that the people of Brentwood saw for nearly two years. However, foraging and skirmishing activities continued and a large force of Federal troops was stationed at Brentwood to protect the vital highway juncture and railroad.

Civil War Skirmishes

The official records of the Civil War reveal that on December 4, 1862, a group of 300 Federal scouts went out from their Nashville stronghold along the Franklin Road, meeting a contingency of Confederate troops which they chased through Brentwood and two miles south of Brentwood on the Wilson Pike. The Federal scouts returned to Brentwood where they were again attacked by Confederates. This time the Confederates were chased through Holly Tree Gap to Franklin.

Five days later, a similar incident occurred on Franklin Road near Holly Tree Gap. Union scouts pursued Southern pickets from Brentwood and fired "several rounds of cannon" at them before returning to Nashville.

During the month of December, 1862, Brentwood became a hot spot of North-South activity. On December 11 and 12 Confederate pickets and a full regiment of men were struck by Union reconnaissance troops on Wilson Pike. After this the Union forces continued down Wilson Pike to Liberty Pike and on to Franklin, which was not officially in Federal hands at that time. Two days later, a Union foraging train was ambushed near Brentwood. The December 21 skirmish with Wharton's Cavalry, which was stationed at Nolensville, on Wilson Pike resulted in six Confederates being captured and one killed. Finally, on December 23, a large Federal wagon train was attacked near Primm's Blacksmith Shop on what is now Crockett Road.

The Civil War also brought spies and Yankee sympathizers to Brentwood. A Union officer wrote to his superior that he had learned from "a citizen named

McCrary of Brentwood" that 500 Rebel cavalry with artillery were camped on Mrs. Hamer's plantation four miles from Brentwood. Mr. McCrary was no doubt a Yankee sympathizer. That location is the farm now owned by T. Vance Little.

Yankee in the Garden

The Saunders family lived on Concord Road near Mill Creek during the Civil War. Yankees camped on nearby Mill Creek. Stanley Owen, a young Union officer, came to forage chickens and hogs at the Saunders farm. He found the yougest daughter, Nancy, working in the garden and stayed to admire her flowers. He came again, and both knew it was love. They eloped, and the family was horrified. Stanley took Nancy home to Illinois where they lived for many years. After Stanley's death, Nancy came home to Williamson County. She is buried in the family cemetery on Concord Road.

Death of the Confederacy

During the first two weeks of December 1864, residents of Brentwood literally saw the death of their beloved Confederacy in battles at each of their neighboring cities: the Battle of Franklin and the Battle of Nashville.

After the Battle of Murfreesboro, the Army of Tennessee ultimately retreated to Chattanooga, where several battles occurred. The Army then made its way to Atlanta for that campaign. By that time General John Bell Hood was in command of the Army of Tennessee. He formulated a plan to lead the army to Nashville and retake the city, then press on to Louisville and Cincinnati. Thus, in the Fall of 1864 Hood's army headed for Nashville. This movement resulted in the Battles of Nashville and Franklin.

When Federal forces heard of Hood's plans, General John M. Schofield and his army were ordered to Nashville from Pulaski where they were stationed to help defend the city. The two armies were in a dead heat for the common destination. Hood had the lead until he camped at Spring Hill on November 29th. Schofield's army passed him and made their way to Franklin where they entrenched themselves.

Hood surveyed the situation from Winstead Hill, south of Franklin, and decided to attack. The battle that followed has been called the bloodiest of the Civil War. Over 6,000 Confederates were killed and wounded. Twelve general officers became casualties: five were killed outright, and one died a few days later.

On the night of November 30, Brentwood residents saw Schofield's army pass along Franklin Road. They had evacuated Franklin and were on their way to Nashville to help in its defense. The next day they saw Hood's army pass in pursuit. He left enough men in Franklin to bury the dead and care for the wounded. The ones who remained set themselves up for battle in the area between Brentwood and Nashville. Hood made his headquarters at Traveler's Rest, just north of Brentwood.

The battle began December 15th and lasted two days, resulting in a devastating defeat for the Army of Tennessee. After it was over, the remnants of the Army of Tennessee retreated along Franklin Road to points south.

In his history of the 20th Tennessee regiment, Dr. McMurray recounts an incident that happened at Brentwood during the aftermath of the Battle of Nashville. The battle was lost, and Hood's army was in full retreat. An effort was made to rally the men at Brentwood, but it was dark and raining. The Federal forces were on Granny White Pike trying to get around Hood's army before they made it to Holly Tree Gap.

In the midst of all this confusion, a young staff officer fresh from furlough arrived on the scene. He urged the men to halt, assuring that there was no danger down there, meaning the battlefield from which they were retreating. An old soldier exhausted from two days of fighting, in rags and with powder burns all over his face, replied, "You go to hell, I've been there."

A force was ordered to cover the retreat at Holly Tree Gap under Forrest, and Hood's army camped for the night all along Franklin Road. Many homes opened their doors to the wounded. It is reported that not a piece of white material was left at Mooreland — sheets, petticoats, and towels were all used to dress wounds.

7
Historic Schools

The first schools in Williamson County were private, possibly plantation schools where tutors were hired to live on the plantation with the family and tutor the children. They may have been what was known as "subscription" schools where a teacher conducted school in his or her home for neighboring children, or several families may have gone together to hire a teacher in a school built for that purpose.

In 1834 a local newspaper ran a notice of a school conducted by a "Miss Bell in her father's home, D. Bell." The father was no doubt David Bell who lived off Edmondson Pike. The school was described as being near the Liberty Meeting House and was said to have about twenty pupils.

Boiling Springs Academy

Boiling Springs Academy opened for classes in 1833 on what is now Moores Lane. The building is still standing. Classes were arranged on three levels with each session lasting five and one half months. The first level taught orthography, reading, writing, and arithmetic and cost eight dollars. The second level consisted of English grammar and geography and cost ten dollars. For fourteen dollars, a student could matriculate in the third level and study Latin, Greek, and the sciences. Boarding students stayed in neighboring homes. J. M. Crown Tilford, the first principal, was a graduate of Cumberland University. The school continued in operation until the early 1900's. The building has also been used as a meeting house for the Presbyterians and other denominations.

Boiling Springs Academy building on Moores Lane.

Lipscomb School

Another well-known school in the Brentwood area is Lipscomb Elementary located on Concord Road. This school has a more illustrious history than one might imagine. It was founded in the late 1860's by William Lipscomb, brother to the founder of David Lipscomb School in Nashville, and former student of Tolbert Fanning, renowned Church of Christ educator of Franklin County, Tennessee.

The first building was a log structure located on the present site of the school. Students came from as far as Kentucky and Alabama and boarded in local homes. After the departure of William Lipscomb, the school degenerated to a one room county school. At that time the school was taken over by the county school system. With the growth of Brentwood, a new building was constructed in 1949. This building burned in 1958 and was replaced in 1959 by the present structure.

8
Historic Churches

Brentwood is fortunate to have over 20 churches within its limits, the vast majority of which are of fairly recent origin. A few churches, however, have been in the Brentwood area for almost as long as it has been settled.

Liberty Methodist Church

No doubt the first church in the Brentwood area was the Liberty Methodist Church. Although located between Brentwood and Nolensville, it became the mother church of churches in both areas. The fact that it was the church of early Brentwood residents is proven by Moore family records which reveal that Eleanor Moore, wife of early Brentwood settler, James Moore, died in 1809 and was buried at the Liberty Meeting House.

The Liberty Church was founded around 1800 by Green Hill, a Revolutionary War veteran and early Methodist leader, who came to Middle Tennessee in the late 1790's to take up a grant on what is now Concord Road. Hill was but one of several early Methodist leaders associated with the Liberty Church. The first trustees of the church included in addition to Green Hill, his son-in-law, Joshua Cannon, also a Methodist preacher; Benjamin Sewell, father of an early Methodist preacher; and Moses Spires (Spier or Spear), another Methodist preacher who came to Middle Tennessee in 1794.

Early Methodist itinerant preacher Lorenzo Dow mentions in his journal attending the Liberty Church in 1804 on his way from Ohio to Natchez, Mississippi. He said:

> Camp meeting commenced at Liberty; here I saw the jerks; and some danced: a strange exercise indeed; however, it is involuntary, yet

Liberty United Methodist Church

requires consent of the will, i.e. the people are taken jerking irresistably, and if they strive to resist it, it worries them much, yet is attended with no bodily pain, and those who are exercised to dance, (which in the pious seems an antodote to the jerks) if they resist, it brings beadness and barrenness over the mind; but when they yield to it they feel happy, although it is a great cross; there is a heavenly smile and solemnity on the countenance, which carries a great conviction to the minds of beholders; their eyes when dancing seem to be fixed upwards as if upon an invisible object, and they are lost to all below.

One of the brightest hours of the Liberty Church was in 1808, when it hosted the Western Conference of the Methodist Church. This conference was presided over by Bishops McKendree and Asbury and was the first annual conference held west of the Alleghenies.

The Liberty Church continues today. Although its membership through the years has never grown much beyond its original number, many of its present members are descendants of its founders.

Brentwood United Methodist Church

The Brentwood United Methodist Church was organized in the 1850's. As no other institution in Brentwood, it has grown with the Brentwood community. Indeed, it takes its beginning, as does the "town" of Brentwood, from the coming of the railroad and the concentration of people in what is now the "town center." The original membership, in addition to new residents, came from two much older churches, Smyrna on the east and Johnson's Chapel on the west. It was originally located on Hardscuffle Road, now Church Street East, near the interstate highway. A two story frame building, the first floor was used for a school and the second floor for church services.

Robert Reams, T. Holmes, H. Oden, D. L. Drake, Stephen Tucker, and Sterling Brown Frost were the first trustees of Brentwood Methodist Church.

Tradition has it that in 1859 the Brentwood Methodist Church broke through the sex barrier. It was the first Methodist Church in the United States to vote to allow men and women to sit together during worship services.

During the Civil War, the church building was confiscated by the Federal Army and used by a large detachment of Federal troops stationed at Brentwood. It was also used as a hospital after the Battle of Nashville. By the end of the war, its greatly delapidated condition reflected its use and abuse during the war.

A colorful wedding took place at the Brentwood Methodist Church during the Civil War. The bride was 24-year-old Mary Hadley, daughter of William and Mary Hadley. Her father had been Felix Grundy's law partner and had served as Mayor of Gallatin.

Mary Hadley was one of six Nashville girls who welcomed the troops of John Bell Hood's Army of Tennessee after their resounding defeat at the Battle of Franklin and before their second humiliation at the Battle of Nashville. Among these troops was Major William Clare, to whom Mary was engaged. They were married 10 days later on December 12, 1864, by Rev. Charles Quintard, an Episcopal chaplain of Hood's army. The couple only had three days to honeymoon before the Battle of Nashville, and most likely spend their time at Mooreland or Traveler's Rest.

During its early years, the Brentwood Methodist Church was unable to support a full-time minister, and was placed on a circuit with other churches, which changed from time to time. Those other churches included Johnson Chapel, Smyrna Church, Thompson's Chapel, and Trinity. Since 1932, Brentwood has been a "single station" church.

In 1884, the Brentwood Church was struck by a windstorm that completely destroyed the building. At that time, a new location on Church Street was donated by Mr. and Mrs. Hugh C. Moore, Sr. The new church, which was next door to what is now the First Tennessee Bank, was dedicated in 1886. On July 11, 1936, tragedy again struck the Brentwood Church when lightening struck the building and burned it to the ground during a violent thunderstorm. Again, the decision was made to rebuild. The new church was dedicated in September 1939. The floors of the new building were made from two giant oak trees that were blown down at the McGavock Hayes farm during the same storm in which the church was destroyed.

Brentwood Church remained on the Church Street site until 1972 when it began to outgrow its physical facility.

Brentwood United Methodist Church moved to its present location in 1972.

Early Brentwood United Methodist Church Pastors

Some early ministers at the Brentwood United Methodist Church and their presiding elders include the following:

Year	District	Presiding Elder	Charge Name	Pastor Appointed
1851	Lebanon	A. L. P. Green	Mill Creek	Geo. W. Winn, John C. Putnam
1852	Lebanon	B. R. Gant	Mill Creek	Lewis C. Bryan, D. C. Kelly
1853	Lebanon	Fountain E. Pitts	Mill Creek	Lewis C. Bryan, J. S. Marks
1854	Lebanon	Fountain E. Pitts	Mill Creek	William Randle, John T. W. Davis
1855	Lebanon	Adam S. Riggs	Mill Creek	Mark W. Clay, Thomas Wainwright
1856	Lebanon	Lewis C. Bryan	Mill Creek	Mark W. Gray
1857	Lebanon	Lewis C. Bryan	Mill Creek	Burkitt F. Ferril, Henry McKinnon
1858	Lebanon	Lewis C. Bryan	Mill Creek	Carroll C. Mayhew, E. Wesley Browning, Martin Clark, Supply.
1859	Lebanon	Lewis C. Bryan	Mill Creek	John J. Comer, William P. Owen
1860	Lebanon	Fountain E. Pitts	Mill Creek	John J. Comer, John A. Jones
1861	Lebanon	John W. Hanner	Mill Creek	William Doss, one to be supplied
1862	Lebanon	John W. Hanner	Mill Creek	William Doss
1863	No session of the Conference because of the Civil War			
1864	Lebanon	John W. Hanner	Mill Creek	Lewis C. Bryan
1866	Lebanon	J. W. Hanner	Mill Creek	L. C. Bryan
1867	Lebanon	David C. Kelley	Mill Creek	William P. Owen
1868	Lebanon	W. Mooney	Mill Creek	J. H. Richardson
1869	Franklin	W. Burr	Harpeth Circuit	J. B. Allison
1870	Franklin	Wm. Burr	Harpeth Circuit	J. B. Allison
1871	Franklin	W. Burr	Brentwood	J. B. Allison
1872	Franklin	W. Burr	Brentwood	J. B. Allison
1873	Franklin	R. P. Ransom	Brentwood Station	J. C. Putman

Brentwood United Methodist Church was situated on the corner of Franklin Road and Church Street until 1972.

Johnson Chapel

Johnson Chapel United Methodist Church traces its history to the early 1800's when settlers came into the Granny White Pike area. Those early settlers included the families of Bond, Owen, Spencer, Mayfield, Carpenter, and Edmiston. Several members of this church are descendants of these families.

The church is thought to have been established in 1803 on a part of the Colonel Thomas McCrory land grant. Major John Johnstone purchased a part of the McCrory grant in 1796. His son, Matthew Johnstone, built the first church on this property. The spelling of the church name through the years has been changed from Johnston to Johnson. The land on which the church was built was deeded to the trustees of the church in 1831. At that time it was used by all denominations.

Before the church building was erected, settlers often held worship services in their homes, and an early minister, Levin Edney, held camp meetings on the McCrory grant. He is thought to be the first minister to hold services at Johnson Chapel.

The first church building was a log structure. In the summer, meetings were often held outdoors on the river bank, and many baptisms were held during the spring and summer months in a deep hole of cool water nearby under a great oak tree. The log church is reported to have burned around 1850. It was replaced with a weather-board building which was razed in 1925.

The present structure was built in 1925. Robert C. Forsythe served as chairman of the building committee, and many church members assisted in the construction of the church, which was designed as a cross. Mrs. Ophelia McClanahan donated many logs for the church, and her son, Lee, hauled them to Junius Morel's sawmill where they were sawed into planks. The structure was dedicated on May 27, 1925.

At the time the new Johnson Chapel Church was built in 1927, the following history of the church was compiled:

Johnson Chapel

HISTORY OF JOHNSON METHODIST CHURCH
BRENTWOOD, TENNESSEE
MAY 17, 1925

For the benefit of future generations, it seems appropriate that we deposit in this corner stone as much of the early history of the church as we may be able to secure.

We can find no record of the exact date of its organization, and must, therefore, rely upon the memories of some of our older members and friends whose grandfathers and grandmothers attended services here.

From the few facts gathered, it is evident that our church has had a most interesting past. If a complete history of it could be written, it would prove most fascinating reading to us of the present time. It is a great pity that no such record has been kept.

From an abstract in the possession of Miss Susie Gardner, we find that about 1831 Matthew Johnston, for whom the church was named, deeded to the trustees the lot on which the church then stood, proving that a building was on the lot at that time.

It is recalled that the original building was in the woods lot just back of the present school building, and probably near the old graveyard in that lot. This was evidently a small building, for we are told that when the revivals were held, they took place in a grove on Little Harpeth on the old Tyler place, now owned by Mr. and Mrs. J. C. Alexander, and was called the "Edney Camp Grounds." At that time people would come from a long distance and camp for days at a time, and were stirred to great religious fervor and enthusiasm.

We infer from the foregoing facts that this has been a religious center and place of worship for over a hundred years.

Some of the early pastors were: Reverends Henry North; Frank Lawrence; A. A. Allison; A. W. Horton; J. J. Pitts; J. B. McFerrin; Hickman; McKinley; Rozelle and Hensley. Bishop Keener also preached here several times during the early years of the church's history.

Harvey Tucker, who has many descendants in this community and elsewhere, was the first superintendent of the Sunday School. He was also one of the original stewards and trustees of the church.

Some of the first members were Harvey Tucker, and wife Mary; Louis Castleman, and wife Eliza; John Lazenby, and wife Sarah; Susan Tucker, formerly Susan Critchlow; J. B. Critchlow, and Adeline Critchlow; Billy Morris; Eliza Carter; a family of Carpenters; W. A. Tucker, and his four sisters whose names were Frances, Mary, Catherine, and Rachel.

At one time the preaching services were held on week days one day each month, and many of the women would walk to church bare-footed, carrying their shoes in their hands and would stop and put them on just before reaching the grounds. They would also bring their knitting with them and knit until preaching began.

While not one of the earliest members, nor a regular pastor of this church, probably no history of it would be complete without reference to a godly man who lived in the community for many years, and who preached here many times, and whose worth and influence was far reaching and recognized by all who knew him. He was Mr. C, or as he was affectionately known by his friends and neighbors, "Cajah Carpenter." He spent much of his time preaching and ministering unto others, and he and Mrs. Carpenter (the latter now living) raised four girls to maturity, and who have also been a great help to the cause of Christ. One daughter, Miss Eva, has for many years been in the foreign fields of India carrying the gospel of our Savior to the heathen lands.

This brings us down to more recent times. About four years ago a young man full of energy and ambition came to us. He found the church disorganized and had the insight to recognize clearly its needs and the courage to put into execution the plans to remedy its defects. Under his able leadership and guidance, there was soon a new interest and enthusiasm manifested in both the church and Sunday School. The various church committees and auxiliaries were revived and put to work. An Epworth League was organized, which is a source of great inspiration to its members and those who attend its services.

This man is Eli C. Shelton, who has labored incessantly for those things tending to our upbuilding and advancement. When he mentioned the importance of a new church, he met but with little encouragement, and where many would have become discouraged and given up, not so with Eli Shelton. Seemingly a defeat merely spurred him on to renewed and greater efforts, until now he is seeing his ambition become a reality. We will doon dedicate to God our new church, and contract a debt of love and gratitude to Eli Shelton, which we and the generations to follow us will never be able to pay. But we rejoice that his reward will be greater than human hands can bestow.

We are indebted to R. C. Tucker, George W. Morgan, Frank G. Gardner, T. M. Cotton, and others for the information and facts contained herein.

May 17, 1925

It is known that Lawrence Evans was compiling the church history and in all probability wrote the corner stone history as above.

102

Owen's Chapel Church of Christ

Owen's Chapel Church of Christ was organized July 24, 1859, and at that time was known as the Euclid Church. The present building was constructed during the 1860's. The bricks were made from clay that came from Owen property east of the church. Slaves who were specially trained as masons in Maryland made the bricks. All of the original roofing, which was brought from England, is still in place except for a portion damaged by a tornado in 1869. The original pews and wooden partition, dividing the sections where the men and women sat, are still intact. Early preachers included David Lipscomb, founder of the Nashville school that bears his name. Church records indicate that at least twice during the Civil War, Sunday services were canceled because Yankees were "foraging in the area."

Owen's Chapel Church of Christ

Smyrna Church

Smyrna Church, founded in 1829 on land given by Captain John Frost, was located near the Frost Cemetery just off Old Smyrna Road. Members of Smyrna Church through the years include the Frost, Herbert, Sneed, Turrentine, Carmichael, Holt, and Williams families. In 1905, Rev. Jeremiah Cullum, the pastor, made the following entry in his journal:

"In the congregation are several very old people. We will soon meet in heaven.

Bro. Wm. Holt, 74, died last week. Henry Edmondson, 77, is feeble and ready. Sister Sallie Williams is 81 — a saint on earth. Rev. A. D. Turrentine, 75, is ready. Bro. Jim P. Sneed, over 70, and his wife, Sister Cornelia Sneed, have their lamps trimmed and burning. Sisters Thenia Edmondson, Elizabeth Holt, Thenia Waller, Mary Hunt Sneed are all on the border land. I know of no other church of its size with so many saintly old people."

The church was disbanded in the late 1930's. At that time, the Brentwood Church was rebuilding after being destroyed by a storm. It was determined that the two churches should combine forces. The Smyrna Church was dismantled and the bricks used to construct the Brentwood Church. Today only the stone where horseback riders dismounted remains in place.

Mt. Lebanon Missionary Baptist Church

Prior to the Civil War, the large black population of Brentwood worshiped on the various plantations or with their masters in "slave galleries" of the white churches. With the end of the War, the blacks became masters of their own fates. One of their first acts in Brentwood was to organize a church. In 1863, Larry Thompson, a Baptist preacher, called together Solomon Pointer, Rob Wilkins, and Lon Hunt to discuss the formation of a church. They met under a large sugar maple tree on Hardscuffle Road and organized the Mt. Lebanon Missionary Baptist Church.

The original membership of the church included the families of Lon and Henry Hunt, Bob Johnson, Bob and Stephen Owens, Robert Daniel, Charles Perkins, Solomon Pointer, and Rob Williams. The first church was located on Hardscuffle Road, now Church Street East. In 1908, the church purchased an abandoned school from the Williamson County Board of Education and remains at this location on Frierson Street.

In 1963, part of the property was taken for the interstate highway. The proceeds were used to build a restroom, a baptistry and an annex.

Brooks Memorial Methodist Church

The Methodist church was important in Brentwood from the earliest days. Most of the white people attended a church of that denomination from settlement until the Civil War. No doubt, the blacks did also; therefore, it was only natural that after the Civil War, the blacks would organize their own Methodist Church. Brooks Memorial was the result of those organizational efforts.

During the first years of its existence, Brooks Memorial Methodist Church shared space with the Mt. Lebanon Baptist Church. In 1935, they acquired three acres on Frierson Street and moved to that location. In 1984, the church moved to a new location in Nashville.

9
Transportation And Communication

Holly Tree Gap

Holly Tree Gap is the gateway to Franklin and the Harpeth Valley. The earliest settlers passed through this gap making their way to new homes. Before the area was settled, scouts went out from Fort Nashboro to explore. In 1797, three such scouts, whom tradition has identified as Graham, Brown, and Tindel, went out with a servant and a dog. They killed a bear, built a fire and were cooking it at Holly Tree Gap when they were attacked and killed by Indians. When a search party went out, they were met by the half-starved dog which led them to the bodies of his slain masters. The search party discovered that the scouts had killed more than their number of Indians.

Controversy exists as to whether the name of this site was originally "Holly Tree" or "Hollow Tree." The early Williamson County Court records refer to it as "Hollow Tree Gap." In later years, these records refer to "Holly Tree Gap." Thomas Hart Benton, the famous Senator from Missouri, lived in Williamson County in the early 1800's and traveled often from Nashville to his home in the Hillsboro community. In his journals, Benton makes reference to a holly tree at the gap, and this reference is often cited by proponents of the name "Holly Tree Gap."

Franklin Road

The Franklin Road (also known as Jackson Highway) was chartered by the Legislature in 1834 and was finished the same year as a "macadamized turnpike." It was built by the Franklin Turnpike Company, and many local residents were investors. Major Thomas Edmondson was superintendent of the construction of the highway. The general route followed the old buffalo trail to the salt licks at Nashville. North of Brentwood, it followed the path of what is now Franklin Pike

Circle and lay east of the highway. In 1928 and 1929, the road was rebuilt to run on the west side of what is now Interstate 65.

Four toll-gates were on the road between Franklin and Nashville, one of which was located at Concord Road and was in operation until the 1920's. The log building which was the toll house still stands.

State and City officials mark the widening of Franklin Road in 1982.

Granny White Pike

Granny White Pike was the main road from Nashville to Franklin until the chartering and construction of the Franklin Turnpike in the 1830's. Many famous men, including such notables as Andrew Jackson, John Coffey, Felix Grundy, John Bell, Matthew Fontaine Maury, and Martin Van Buren traveled what was known as the middle road in the early days.

Thomas Hart Benton, one of the more famous travelers, gave the road its name and made it nationally known. His family settled at Old Hillsboro in Williamson County in 1800 on a 2,500-acre grant. He became a lawyer and was admitted to the bar in Franklin in the first decade of the 1800's. His legal work and friendship with Andrew Jackson made it necessary for him to travel frequently to Nashville. In doing so, he would stop at a tavern or inn along the way operated by Lucinda White, a widow from North Carolina. Benton and others were impressed with Mrs. White's fare and with her frugality and industry.

Some years later, Thomas Hart Benton moved to Missouri, where he was elected to the U.S. Senate. He served for more than twenty-five years in that body and became one of the most influential politicians in America. Once in a speech before the Senate, he was pleading for perpetuation of the American ideals of freedom, independence, and hard work. He used Granny White, who ran an humble inn on the Middle Road out of Nashville, as an example of the embodiment of these virtues. She became a celebrity as a result of this recognition, and has been immortalized by having the road named for her.

In the early 1840's, Granny White Pike came close to being transformed into a major thoroughfare into Nashville. Efforts were being made to form a new turnpike company and improve the old road from Nashville to Franklin, "commonly called the Middle or Granny White Road." These efforts were opposed, no doubt, by the principals of the Franklin Turnpike Company, which had been chartered and built ten years before. Lobbying activities convinced the Williamson County Court to adopt a resolution addressed to the Tennessee State Legislature opposing the formation of the new company. A petition dated October 4, 1847, signed by all the members of the Williamson County Court, stated that ". . . the convenience and welfare of the people generally of this county does not require the construction of another turnpike road . . ." The petition further stated that they wanted to reserve for the people "the privilege" of traveling the old road.

Wilson Pike

Wilson Pike was chartered in the 1840's as the Harpeth Turnpike. It was named for James Hazard Wilson, the first president of the turnpike company. There is no more historic stretch of road in the South than Wilson Pike, which extends from

Brentwood south to the community of Arrington on Highway 96.

Stately plantation homes line this road even though time is beginning to obscure their secrets. On a thirteen-mile stretch of road there is said to have been thirteen murders. Stories range from two brothers getting into an argument over which one their mother had told to drive a calf out of the yard to an argument that arose over fox hunters chasing a fox into the basement of one of the plantation homes.

No tale is quite so poignant as the one told by a tombstone in the Standfield cemetery on the old Tulloss farm at Clovercroft. The inscription reads: "Spivey Standfield, born October 1809, murdered by Bill and Sam Wilson, died September 17, 1841."

In 1847 the residents along the Harpeth Turnpike presented a petition to the Tennessee General Assembly concerning the location of a toll gate on the pike. The toll gate was originally scheduled to be installed at a point one mile from the northern terminus of the pike, where James Green now lives. The directors of the company wanted to move the toll gate two miles south of the terminus, approximately the southern boundary of Carondelet Subdivision. The residents turned out in force to oppose the two mile site.

The petition stated that traffic in the area moved south, to Franklin where the courts were and to McDaniel's and Reed's plantations where the polling places were, as well as to Elmwood to church. It was pointed out that the only traffic going north was that going to Nashville. From this petition, it is apparent that there was nothing at what is now the town center of Brentwood.

Signers of the petition included: James Johnston, C. McDaniel, Laban Walters, D. P. Hadly, Turner Williams, Peter Owen, Jesse H. Phillips, William L. Sneed, S. B. Frost, Daniel Carmack, John Edmondson, Robert N. Herbert, David Bell, R. R. Hightower, William L. Robards, Pierce Waller, Nathan Owen, and Everett Owen.

The Railroads

The first railroad was built through Brentwood in the 1850's, and the first train passed through in 1859. At that time the cut was only 15 feet deep, and the trains had to ascend a steep grade to reach Brentwood. The original train station was on the south side of Church Street near the site of what is now Nashville City Bank. The track was slightly west of where the present tracks are located, and was originally the property of the Tennessee and Alabama Railroad, which in 1866 became the Nashville and Decatur Railroad Company. The Louisville and Nashville Railroad Company acquired the line in 1871.

The present cut, which is 74 feet deep and ½-mile long, was completed in 1912, and the railroad station was moved to the point where the railroad crosses Old Smyrna Road. Workers on this project had to chip through solid stone to complete the cut. They lived in small houses along what is now Brentwood's town center.

The Franklin Interurban Railroad

For over 32 years, electric trolley cars ran through Brentwood on their way to and from Nashville and Franklin. Workers, shoppers, and students were regular riders. The first run of these small cars was on April 24, 1909, and the last run was on November 9, 1941. The route crossed Franklin Road at many points, and also passed through what is now Meadow Lake Subdivision and the Brentwood Country Club. There was a substation on Franklin Road where Rhea Little's Shell Station now stands, which over the years was manned by Morton Carpenter, Jeff Shockley, Doc McCord, and Aleck Bradford.

Other Roads

Old Hickory Boulevard between Granny White Pike and Edmondson Pike was completed in 1936. Concord Road was originally called Callendar Lane, named for the Callendar family whose home stood on the road at the point where the railway first crossed it. Church Street East was known as Hardscuffle Road, taking its name from the rocky area east of Brentwood, and ran all the way to Edmondson Pike via the eastern portion of what is now called Cloverland Drive.

WSM Radio Tower

Possibly the most familiar landmark in Brentwood today is the WSM Radio Tower. When it was built, it was the second tallest tower in the world, being exceeded in height only by the Eiffel Tower in Paris. WSM is one of a very few "clear channel" radio stations, meaning that it encounters a minimum of interference on the 650 frequency. At night WSM can be heard throughout the United States and covers more area than any other radio station in America.

The site for the WSM Radio Tower was chosen because of soil conditions as well as geographic location. The concrete supports go the the bedrock in the area. The eight cables holding the tower are 2½ inches in diameter and weigh 8,000 pounds each. The tower is 804 feet tall and can carry 50,000 watts.

The Post Office

Tradition has it that the first post office to serve the Brentwood Area (long before the area was known as Brentwood) was located on the Frost property on Old Smyrna Road, also the site of Mayfield Station. Before that time, this location was the site of an Indian town. Even though postal records show no evidence of a

The Franklin Interurban Railroad was completed in 1908. A ceremony commemorating its completion was held in Franklin and was hosted by Henry Hunter Mayberry, president of the railroad company. His daughter handed a golden spike to Franklin mayor E. M. Perkens to be driven as the last spike in the railroad between Franklin and Nashville.

The organization of the Interurban was almost universally opposed. Franklin and Brentwood merchants foresaw themselves losing customers to the better shopping areas of Nashville. Toll gate operators on Franklin Road foresaw a serious loss of revenue. The Franklin chapter of the Daughters of the Confederacy was strongly opposed to the encirclement of the town's Confederate monument on the stone square by steel rails and bright yellow trolley cars. Finally, no small objection to overcome was the acquisition of the right-of-way over lands whose owners felt that their privacy was being invaded.

In Brentwood, the Interurban crossed the lands of the McGavock family, the Hayes family, and the Mizell family, as well as the lands which are now occupied by the Baptist Children's Home, the Brentwood Country Club, and Meadow Lake subdivision. It stopped at Concord Road (then called Callendar Lane), and in Meadow Lake. The small stand where it stopped in Meadow Lake can still be seen.

In spite of the objections, the Interurban made its maiden run on Christmas Eve, 1908. It remained in business until after World War II.

WSM Tower on Concord Road.

post office in the early days, the Frost property would have been the logical place for it since it was the site of the local general store and grist mill.

The Good Spring Post Office, established April 24, 1827, was the first official post office to serve the Brentwood area (also before it was called Brentwood). Colin McDaniel, who lived at what is now Stonehenge Subdivision, was the postmaster at that station. He was succeeded in 1847 by James M. Reed. The post office itself was located on what is now the Country Club property.

The first post office to bear the name "Brentwood" was established August 8, 1856 and was located on the corner of Wilson Pike and Old Smyrna Road. The building now stands in the yard of the home of the late Mary Sneed Jones on Wilson Pike, across the road from where it originally stood.

Brentwood's first post office building, situated in the yard of Valley View Farm on Wilson Pike.

After the post office was moved from Old Smyrna Road and Wilson Pike, it occupied variously the stores of Hillary Crockett, Arnold Anderson, Rizerdorf Harriman, and Dan Leeds. In 1937 it was moved to the Franklin Road side of town and occupied several locations before settling in 1956 in a small building constructed by Mr. Glenn Noble and his sister Mrs. Richard Frank, now the site of the Franklin Road Liquor Store. The post office later moved to another Franklin Road location, the present site of the Campus Computer Store. However, the subsequent growth of Brentwood made larger quarters necessary, and a new post office was built on Church Street. That facility too has been outgrown, and the newest postal building is located on Brook's Chapel Road.

The first rural route to be run from the post office was made by Sam Taylor in 1902. This route was later expanded to three routes, handled for many years by Frank Morgan, John Sawyer, and Walter Lamb. Later the three routes were decreased to two, with route one on the east side of Franklin Road and route two on the west side. Mr. and Mrs. Marion Oden both served for many years as the mail couriers, as did Walter D. Ragsdale.

Since the founding of the Brentwood post office in 1856, the following persons have served as its postmasters:

George W. Simpson	August 8, 1856
Charles T. Cleland	February 19, 1866
James H. M. Hall	August 21, 1867
William P. Newland	April 29, 1872
John N. Simpson	October 13, 1881
James T. Williams	April 2, 1890
John T. Anderson	November 26, 1890
William M. Carr	January 28, 1902
James A. Carr (declined)	November 19, 1903
Hilary R. Crockett	April 21, 1904
Addison L. Edmunds	June 8, 1922
Risedorf E. Harriman	September 27, 1926
Marion F. Oden	January 25, 1935
Mrs. Mae J. Redmon	September 1, 1942
Mrs. Dorothy Duffield Bobo	July 8, 1944
Charles R. Sheler	May 16, 1946
Alva E. Duffield	June 16, 1947
Richard Dotson	January 31, 1976
William L. Foster	September 29, 1984

Post office built by Glenn Noble. The building now forms the center portion of Franklin Road Wine and Liquors.

Brentwood's new post office, completed in 1984.

10
Maryland Farms

No organization or institution has been more influential in setting the pace for Brentwood's lifestyle than Maryland Farms. The institution began as a pacesetter. For many years, the name Brentwood was synonymous with fine-blooded horses. So was the name Maryland Farms.

Maryland Farms had its beginning in 1937 when J. Truman Ward, then the owner of WLAC Radio Station in Nashville, bought 100 acres of stump land along Old Hickory Boulevard near the village of Brentwood. He later added other acreage, making Maryland Farms, named for his wife, Mary, a 400-acre spread unsurpassed in the South.

Ward's love for horses manifested itself in this showplace for fine horses. He began by building a twenty-stall stable measuring 44 by 155 feet with an interior of wormy chestnut and knotty pine ceilings. Twenty by twenty foot stalls were finished in oak. Both American saddle horses and Tennessee walking horses were stabled there in the beginning for training. Other barns and pastures enclosed within the farm's five-mile white fence were home to 50 brood mares.

American Ace

In 1941 Ward bought seven mares and a stallion named American Ace, who achieved worldwide fame as an outstanding show performer, from Spindletop Farm in Lexington, Kentucky. American Ace was the leading sire of his breed in the late 1940's. He died in 1953.

Many notables visited Maryland Farms. Some who bought its horses were Gene Autry, Barbara Stanwyck, and Norrie Goff of the radio team "Lum and Abner." Also, industrialist Victor Emanuel came to purchase horses and remained to locate a plant at Nashville, Vultee Aircraft Corporation, now AVCO.

J. Truman Ward, founder of Maryland Farms, with American Ace.

Maryland Manor, the Ward residence, was built in 1941-42. The two-story Colonial-style structure was built in fine architectural style of classic design and featured over 7,500 feet of living space.

After the death of American Ace, the Ward family replaced their horse operation with a cattle farm boasting over 200 head of Hereford cattle. In 1958, Maryland Farms once again became a horse farm, this time by lessee Edward Potter, founder and president of Commerce Union Bank and the Tennessee Thoroughbred Training Association, of which he was president. A three-eights mile covered training track was moved from the Tennessee State Fairgrounds to Maryland Farms. There was also a five-eights mile open track. During this period, there were over 100 horses in training at Maryland Farms. Middle Tennessee weather was deemed ideal for this type of operation.

Among the many dignitaries who visited Maryland Farms were Mr. and Mrs. Andy Devine, shown with Mrs. Ward (left) and Truman Ward (right).

An aerial view of Maryland Farms in 1940.

Hallway and reception room in the show barn at Maryland Farms.

Maryland Manor in the days when it was a cattle farm.

A Vision

By 1968, Brentwood had become more than a sleepy village at the hub of what had been plantation homes and more or less prosperous tobacco farms. It became an incorporated city in 1969 and was experiencing a variety of growing pains as well as criticism by those who opposed growth. Truman Ward and his son, Jimmy, had a vision. They saw a community where there had been a horse farm. They saw office buildings in a garden-type suburban environment. They saw research facilities, banks, and company headquarters. They saw hotels, recreational facilities, tree-lined streets and flower beds. They saw a shopping center and residential development. They saw a new Brentwood, and that dream has largely come true.

From a horse farm to an office complex, Maryland Farms continues to provide community leadership.

11
The Renaissance

Most of Brentwood's mansions, if not its way of life, survived the Civil War. As we have seen it was in the best interest of Federal occupiers to keep these plantations intact because their produce fed and supported the armies of the intruders. Although the houses themselves survived, the way of life they represented vanished. Entire plantations fell into ruin and decay. Families who were unable to support themselves on their land either moved away in search of new beginnings or clung hopelessly to a way of life sustained only by memories.

Rediscovery

In the first half of this century, the great homes and fine farms of Brentwood were rediscovered. Brentwood's proximity to Nashville made it an ideal location for those who possessed the financial resources to move to this suburban location.

There were two primary reasons for the renewed interest in Brentwood. Undoubtedly, the local historic homes which could be restored appealed strongly to prospective residents. The Stirton Omans purchased and remodeled Ashlawn. The C. P. Wilsons bought and restored Mountview in 1924. In the 1940's, the John Omans bought the old Johnston house, named it Thurso, and restored it to its former grandeur. It was later renamed Isola Bella. Green Pastures was purchased and restored to its original condition by the Mason Houghlands in the 1930's. Century Oak was owned by Edward Potter. The Vernon Sharps purchased Inglehame in 1938. Frank Gasser purchased Clover Lawn in 1927. Other notable families who moved to Brentwood during the renaissance include the John Sloan, Sr. family, who purchased Maple Grove Farm in 1940 from Owen Allen and built upon it the house in which they still reside. The T.P. Kennedy's, the Marshall Derryberrys, the William Puryears, the Arthur J. Dyers, and the Charles Plaxicos also were among the families who moved to Brentwood during this period.

Prior to 1950, the widespread interest in housing development that characterizes

Brentwood today had not emerged. However, there is no doubt that, even prior to 1950, discerning people were discovering Brentwood's beneficial qualities. Their movement into the area foreshadowed the surge in local growth which followed.

Also significant in attracting new residents to the area were Brentwood's major equestrian events, notable horse shows and fox hunts, which captured the imagination of a special group of new residents who moved to Brentwood in the early part of this century and thus brought about a "renaissance" in the area.

Horses

Since the remote day when Tennessee was young, horses have been plentiful and in great number here. Tennesseans have always loved horses — this is not unnatural, for the population is predominantly Anglo-Saxon. Englishmen have always loved and raced their horses. Further, the Central Basin of Tennessee is a "natural" for all types of livestock. The native bluegrass, the gently rolling hills, the varied species of trees and the numerous springs all contribute to the production and development of fine horses. Horses foaled here grow rapidly and possess great stamina due to the phosphate and lime content of the soil. It has been observed that native Tennessee horses are remarkably free from blemishes and unsoundness, a by-product of the mineral-rich environment.

When the early Tennessee settlers came across the mountains from Virginia and the Carolinas to build homes in the newfound wilderness, they brought their horses with them. These horses were a sturdy breed of saddlers, and there were thoroughbred stallions among them. According to the earliest records available, breeders and thoroughbreds were prominent in Middle Tennessee. These horses played an important role in the development of the Tennessee Pacer and the Tennessee Walking Horse. Today, hundreds of horses within a 75-mile radius of Nashville flourish in a variety of stables, barns, and open pastures. They are "at home" here, and have been so for more than a hundred years.

The Iroquois Steeplechase. — Touted for many years as "the South's Greatest One-Day Sporting Event," the Iroquois Steeplechase is held near Brentwood in Nashville's Percy Warner Park on the Saturday in May following the Kentucky Derby. The prestige surrounding this event has conferred the name "Iroquois Day" on the day of this event, an annual tradition since 1941. The main event has been run continuously since 1941 with only one break, in 1945, because of the war. It has from the beginning attracted horses and riders of class and distinction. The number of starters in the main event has varied, from five in 1944 to 16 in 1950. During recent years, large fields have been the rule.

The first Iroquois Steeplechase meeting in 1941 had only five races, but there was no shortage of either entries or spectators even at the first meeting. Approximately 40,000 people witnessed a spectacle which had never before come to Middle Tennessee, one which has subsequently become the best steeplechase in the world, apart from infield races at major tracks.

A great deal of tradition seems to have become full-blown at the time of the first meeting. The race is named in honor of Iroquois, the only American-bred three year old ever to win the prestigious Epson Derby in England, which he did in 1881.

The Iroquois was a pioneer in the upsurge of steeplechasing which has swept the South and West. Within a year after the first Iroquois meeting, other similar meetings began to be held in Peoria, Illinois, Tryon, North Carolina, Chicago, St. Louis, Indianapolis, and Louisville.

Horses of Maryland Farms. — As previously mentioned, one of the most out-standing horse nurseries in the south was Brentwood's own Maryland Farms, which is now an office complex. Located on Old Hickory Boulevard nine miles south of Nashville, this beautiful farm of 317 acres was ideally situated in the foothills of the Harpeth Valley.

Maryland Farms was owned by Mr. and Mrs. J. Truman Ward, who shared a life-long love of horses. Their son, Jim, acquired their love for horses, and took as much interest in them as did his parents. Maryland Farms is named for Mrs. Ward, whose given name was Mary. The Ward family derived much pleasure as well as notable success from their farm and saddle horse operation. They had one of the most attractive show and training stables in the country, surrounded by miles of white board fences, paddocks, stately trees, and pastures. Especially noteworthy was their barn, which was built along colonial lines.

The barn at Maryland Farms, remodeled as an office building.

Maryland Farms attracted numerous persons who were interested in both American Saddle Horses and Tennessee Walking Horses. A great variety of horses was available at Maryland Farms, from weanling colts to finished horses ready for the show ring, not to mention well-trained pleasure horses of both breeds.

Over forty top-blooded brood mares were stabled at Maryland Farms, many of which established outstanding show records before being retired. The farm boasted three prize sires, including the nationally famous American Ace, purchased by Mr. Ward from Spindletop Farms in Lexington, Kentucky.

Although no longer in operation as a horse farm, Maryland Farms today continues its heritage of leadership as an office park in which numerous corporations house their national headquarters.

The Brentwood Derby. —From 1959 until 1971, Maryland Farms was the site of the annual Brentwood Derby, a local horse racing event. Edwin C. Eggert developed an interest in horse racing and persuaded the Brentwood Chamber of Commerce to promote the Derby as a fund-raising event. In addition to Eggert, the first committee to oversee the event included Irby Bright, Bob Smith, Harry Pearson, and Eddie Arnold. The Derby was the only fund-raising event sponsored by the Chamber of Commerce during the days of its running, and revenues from the event were used to support charitable organizations and civic projects. Among these were the National Kidney Foundation, Fanny Battle Day Home, Lipscomb School Library, Granberry School Library, Crippled Children's Hospital, Little League Baseball, the Boy Scouts of America, and the Girl Scouts of America. The last Derby was held on April 24, 1971.

The Brentwood Horse Show. — Starting first at Robertson Academy and later moving to the Houghland family's Bright Hour Farm, the Brentwood Horse Show was an annual event where horse owners and their families gathered for fun and competition. Especially noteworthy in connection with this event was the Vernon Sharp family, who won the event more often than did any of the other participants. Calvin Houghland, Jr. reports that many present-day residents of Brentwood and Nashville often refer to their participation in the event. A similar event was held at Maryland Farms in the 1940's.

Hounds

The Harpeth Hills Hunt Club. — In the early 1920's, Rogers Caldwell and a group of friends organized the Harpeth Hills Hunt Club. The long club house was situated on Old Hickory Boulevard. In traditional English style, the club organized and held fox hunts. Harpeth Hills Hunt Club disbanded in 1938, several years after some of its main supporters had organized another similar club known as the Hillsboro Hounds.

The Hillsboro Hounds. — Formed in 1932 by a group of Harpeth Hills Hunt Club members, the Hillsboro Hounds named themselves after the nearby town of Hillsboro. Original members were Mason Houghland, James Stahlman, Edward Potter, and John Sloan, Sr. The Hillsboro Hounds were organized on a subscription basis, meaning that participants subscribed in order to take part in club-sponsored hunts. A club restriction was that the Hillsboro Hounds would never own a club house. Kennels for the club hounds were at Green Pastures.

For a number of years, the club conducted its hunts in Boston, a small town south of Brentwood, and later they began to hunt in the Greenbriar area, north of Nashville. During this period, the horses and hounds were kept in the Nelson Whiskey Warehouse in Greenbriar. In 1938, the hunts returned to the Brentwood area. The Hillsboro Hounds still exist, and continue to hold fox hunts throughout the Middle Tennessee area.

Mason Houghland
Master, Hillsboro Hounds

John Sloan, Sr.
Secretary, Hillsboro Hounds

Horses of Maryland Farms in the 1940's.

12
Historic Businesses

Brentwood today is a rapidly growing business area. Numerous companies, such as Murray Ohio and Service Merchandise, have located their national headquarters here. Other businesses function daily, providing products and services for a wide territory.

Notable Businesses of the Past

Notable businesses no longer in existence served as institutions in Brentwood. These businesses will be remembered by long-time Brentwood residents, but most of Brentwood's current population is probably unaware that they ever existed or were important.

Leeds Store. — Leeds Store, long a landmark on the corner of Church Street and Wilson Pike, was opened in 1931 by Daniel Lake Leeds, who moved to Brentwood from Philadelphia. After the marriage of his daughter, Mary Vena, to Floyd W. Jones, he and his son-in-law operated the store as a partnership under the name Leeds and Jones until the store closed in 1956. It was a general merchandise store, selling groceries, feed, horseshoe nails, and sundry other items. It was also a Saturday night meeting place for the older people to gather and listen to the Grand Ole Opry. The post office was also located in Leeds Store for several years.

Gooch Television Service. — After retiring from Major League Baseball in 1942 and from the baseball bat manufacturing business in 1947, John B. (Johnny) Gooch started a small business in 1953 designing and marketing wood lamps, candle holders, tables, etc. made of the finest woods, hand-turned and beautifully finished, which he made himself. His shop was located on the east side of Franklin Road in Brentwood in a building that housed the Brentwood Hardware on the north portion of the building. The shop was on the south end between the

Brentwood Hardware and the alley which divided the building and Pewitt's Service Station. This area is now occupied by the First American National Bank.

In the latter part of 1953, his son, Beverly R. Gooch, began Gooch Television Service in the south half of the shop. Beverly serviced televisions, radios, electronic amplifiers of country music stars, and built and sold large stereo systems and other related electronics. Here Beverly also invented an Audio-Video Tape Recorder which used ¼-inch tape. Young Gooch remained in the television business from 1953-1956 when he had to move because the dust and vibrations from his father's woodworking interfered with the delicate electronics. He moved to his laboratory in the Formosa Building on Hillsboro Road in Green Hills, where he remained until 1959 when he sold his invention and left Nashville.

Johnny Gooch remained in the woodworking business at the same site until 1964 when he moved to a smaller shop immediately behind the first one. He remained there until June, 1974, when he retired altogether. This small shop was located at the present site of the tall Exxon sign and the parking area for the bank. The shops were rented from Howard Gardner.

Historic Businesses Still in Existence

Twenty-five years ago, businesses in Brentwood were few in number. Those among them still surviving number only seven: Noble's Restaurant, Traveler's Rest Motel, Pewitt's Service Station, Huff's Market, Barbara's House of Beauty (now known as The Hair Studio), Brentwood Barber Shop, and Star Market.

Noble's Restaurant. — The oldest Brentwood business still in existence is Noble's. In 1929, A. H. (Albert) Noble purchased approximately five acres on the corner of Franklin Road and Old Hickory Boulevard for the "enormous" sum of $5,000.00. A registered pharmacist, Noble opened a drug store on the site. Marion Oden, also a registered pharmacist, assisted him in the business.

Noble's remained a drug store until 1947, when Glenn Noble and his wife opened a restaurant in the building. In 1949, the Nobles sold the restaurant but retained ownership of the building. For many years, Noble's was the only restaurant in Brentwood. The restaurant has subsequently been owned and operated by several persons.

Traveler's Rest. — Traveler's Rest Motel was built adjacent to Noble's Restaurant by Glenn Noble in 1953. For over 30 years, the Noble family has managed the motel as a lodging place for families and business people. No other landmarks in Brentwood are as identifiable to newcomers as are these two time-honored businesses.

Pewitt's Exxon. — In 1938, Emery Pewitt and his brother Luther opened a garage and service station on Franklin Road where The Odyssey Salon is now located.

The new business flourished, and the Pewitt brothers did all the work themselves.

When World War II was declared, neither Emery nor Luther was accepted for military service, but they left their business and went to work in an aircraft factory in Alabama, training new workers in airplane repair and mechanical work.

In 1944, the Pewitt brothers returned to Brentwood and went back to their garage. In 1949 they moved to a new location, which was on Franklin Road in a building formerly operated as The Palms nightclub.

Adopting a policy of never closing, Pewitt Brothers Service Station offered complete mechanical repair, gasoline, oil, and lawn mower repair. Being open all night seems to have been an open invitation to petty thieves and hold-up men. In 1941, an employee named Aaron Furlough was help up by a lone gunman and locked in a restroom. His cries for help summoned Emery Pewitt. As the two were searching the area, a movement in the bushes prompted Emery Pewitt to fire his gun, killing a dog. The thief escaped with $30 and an electric razor.

In the mid-sixties, the Pewitts built the present Exxon station. They located it behind the old station in anticipation that Franklin Road would one day be widened — perhaps the best long-range planning in Brentwood up to that time. Their judgment proved correct, as Franklin Road was expanded to four lanes many years later.

During the blizzard of 1951, their station remained open when most other businesses were closed. During the calamity, their station proved to be a true "service station," as they helped to deliver food and fuel to stranded families. They also kept the WSM radio station on the air by means of a makeshift power lawnmower motor.

Emery Pewitt served as Brentwood's first mayor.

Huff's Market. — Huff's Market began in Brentwood in 1949. Glenn Huff, its founder, was no stranger to the grocery business, having worked with his father in a grocery in Burwood.

Glenn Huff stated that he was hauling bricks to build Trinity School and frequently stopped by a small grocery on Wilson Pike in Brentwood to buy his lunch. The owners proposed to sell the store to Huff and he purchased it. At the beginning, the store had an inventory of $2,200.00 and a truck valued at $400.00.

Many of Huff's customers were black people who lived in the area known as Hardscuffle, now called Church Street. On many occasions, Huff allowed people to sign tickets for food when they had no money. As he looks back, he affirms that while he may have occasionally not been paid for items sold on credit, he has been providentially rewarded for his willingness to help needy people.

Huff recalls the prices on some items when he opened the store. Pink salmon sold for a dime a can. Cold drinks were a nickle each and nineteen cents for a six-pack. Hamburger and ground beef were 39 cents a pound. It was after Huff came to Brentwood that coffee prices rose above 25 cents per pound, and when it later went to 49 cents a pound, people began saying they were going to quit drinking coffee altogether. Cigarettes were 20 cents a pack.

Huff rented the building for his grocery business for 12 years, then purchased it. Over the years, he also purchased land across the street from the store. On August 2, 1983, a new and larger Huff's was built on that site. During the construction of the new store, two construction workers, unaware of who the owner of the new store was, went over to Huff's old store to purchase lunch. While they were eating, Huff overheard one of them say, "When that new store across the street opens up, this little place will have to go out of business!" Indeed it did — as a grocery. And Huff's new store across the street continues to grow. Management of that growth is done mostly by Mike Huff, co-owner of the store.

Barbara's House of Beauty. — In 1956, Barbara Campbell, daughter of Mr. and Mrs. Emery Pewitt, started a beauty shop in the garage of her home on what is now Pewitt Drive. In 1963, the business began to expand, adding an operator each year until 1967. At that time, the family moved out of the house and it was used exclusively for the business. Remodeling was completed in 1967, to make the building appear substantially as it does today. In 1974, Mrs. Campbell sold the business but retained ownership of the property. In 1982, she sold the property as well to Mrs. Rita Johnson Chidlow. The shop was renamed The Hair Studio in 1984.

Brentwood Barber Shop. — The Brentwood Barber Shop was begun by Bobby Rutledge in 1957. The first location was on Franklin Road by the Shell station, but later moved to another location on Franklin Road adjacent to Pewitt's Exxon. In 1972, the barber shop moved again to a new building at the corner of Church Street (then Hardscuffle) and Wilson Pike Circle, where it exists today.

Star Market. — Located next door to Pewitt's Exxon station, Star Market began operation in 1959. The Pewitt family has maintained ownership of the property, while other entrepreneurs have maintained the business. Mrs. Yvonne Troxler operated the Star Market from 1960 until 1983, when it was purchased by Sang Yi, its current owner.

At this writing, Brentwood is being "invaded" by innumerable businesses. Office buildings, once rare, are being constructed at an unprecedented rate. Retail outlets continue to multiply. With the recent announcement of the coming of General Motors' Saturn Plant to nearby Spring Hill, Brentwood seems destined to forsake its rural roots in favor of becoming a bustling business district. However, Brentwood residents expect to maintain their current high standards for quality of life thanks to a Master Land Use Plan created by the Brentwood Planning Commission.

Glenn Huff, his wife Honor, and their sons Mike (left) and Terry (right).

Glenn Huff, veteran grocery manager.

Huff's delivery truck in the early days of operation.

Huff's Market, built in 1983.

The interior of Noble's Pharmacy (upper). Noble's began operation as a restaurant in 1948 (lower left). A. H. Noble, founder of Noble's Pharmacy (lower right).

134

Noble's in 1941.

Traveler's Rest Motel has been in operation continuously since 1953.

Emery and Luther Pewitt's first business location. Left to right are: Luther Pewitt, Emery Pewitt, and Clyde Campbell, Jr. (upper). The second location of Pewitt Brothers Garage, originally the site of the Palms Nightclub (lower left). Present Pewitt Exxon (lower right).

Brentwood Barber Shop in 1958.

Home of Barbara Campbell, which later became Barbara's House of Beauty.

Barbara's House of Beauty, now known as The Hair Studio.

13
City Government

On April 15, 1969, the citizens of Brentwood, recognizing the imminent growth of the community, voted to incorporate the city. Concurrent with the incorporation was the adoption of the commission-manager form of government. The following June 3, the citizens went to the polls again and elected commissioners to oversee the development of the community.

The structure of the commission-manager government is similar to that of a large business corporation. The voters, like stockholders of a corporation, elect the board of directors; in the case of the city, the board of commissioners. The board of commissioners then elect from their number a mayor, whose position is similar to the chairman of the board. The board of commissioners also chooses a city manager, whose duties compare to those of a business corporation general manager.

The Board of Commissioners

Five commissioners are elected at large for staggered four year terms. Their functions include:
- Adopting and amending city ordinances and resolutions.
- Determining city policies and standards of service.
- Determining how much money is spent and for what purposes.
- Determining what city taxes are to be levied.
- Approving contracts, agreements, and bids.
- Appointing citizens to various boards and committees.
- Representing the municipality as its political leadership.

The Mayor

The Mayor is a co-equal commission member who is elected by majority vote of the commission as its chairman for a two-year term. The mayor presides at each meeting of the commission and executes all deeds, bonds, and contracts made in the name of the city. A vice-mayor is chosen in the same manner and presides in the absence of the mayor.

Emery Pewitt was Brentwood's first mayor. Brian Joe Sweeney has served longer in the office than any other mayor.

The City Manager

The city manager is appointed by the board of commissioners for an indefinite term. The city manager serves as the chief administrative officer and is responsible for carrying out the policies adopted by the board of commissioners. As chief administrative officer of the city, the manager is empowered to make all personnel appointments, supervise the work of all departments, enforce the laws and ordinances of the city, prepare and recommend an annual budget to the board of commissioners, and administer the day to day business of the city.

The Planning Commission

The planning commission is responsible for approval of all new subdivisions of land within the city and the construction of new roads and utilities to serve these developments. They also approve all new building sites within the various commercial districts of the city. Zoning ordinances and changes in zoning are studied and recommended to the board of commissioners for action. The commission is composed of eight citizens of the city appointed by the city manager, a member elected from the board of commissioners, and the city manager.

The Board of Zoning Appeals

The Board of Zoning Appeals interprets zoning ordinances and makes allowances for changes as necessary. This body is the final authority in the settlement of zoning disputes.

The Library Board

The Brentwood Library Board is composed of six citizens appointed by the city manager and one city commissioner appointed by the board of commissioners. The library is located in the Buchanan House, situated on Franklin Road, which was built in 1925. In 1985, renovation of the library was completed, allowing for expansion of resources and community services.

Sister Cities Board

Brentwood is involved in the Sister Cities Program and has formed a relationship with its counterpart in Brentwood, England. A board of citizens and commissions oversee this program.

Growing Pains

When Brentwood incorporated, both the water services and fire services were provided by private enterprise. In 1981, Brentwood acquired the water department and has since expanded its services. The city assumed responsibility for fire department services in 1985.

Because of the rapid growth of the city, Brentwood has in times past found itself with a shortage of water. Action to correct this problem has been taken with the addition of more storage tanks and the forming of agreements with neighboring Nashville for supplies of water.

Future Development

At this writing, there remain 9,800 acres undeveloped out of the total 23,040 acres in Brentwood. This land is subject to intense development pressures. Thus, the planning commission and board of commissioners developed a master land use plan. The importance of this study is highlighted by the fact that zoning and development have been sources of controversy in Brentwood since (and even before) incorporation.

The master land use plan advocates a "managed" growth policy based on (1) maintaining an average density of one dwelling unit per acre, (2) moderating the growth rate so as to match the community's capacity to provide services, and (3) preserving open space through public acquisition, restriction of development on unsuitable soils and topography and incentives for private provisions.

Brentwood's first city hall on Pewitt Drive is now a Chinese restaurant.

Brentwood Municipal Building.

City Commissioners

Since incorporating the city in 1969, the citizens of Brentwood have elected 20 residents to serve as city commissioners. For each term, the commissioners elect a mayor. Commissioners who have served as mayor are indicated by an asterisk (*).

Emery C. Pewitt
1969-1970*

Bob Robinson
1969-1970

John E. Sloan, Jr.
1969-1972*

W. Allen Bryan III
1971-1972

Reuben E. Harris
1971

James T. Redd
1972

Thomas E. Midyett, Jr.
1972-1977

Brian Joe Sweeney
1972-1985*

R. C. Bailey
1973-1976

Raymond L. Weiland
1973-1976*

Jack Green
1973-1976

Thomas H. Bain
1977-1980

William H. McCord
1977-1980

Guilford F. Thornton
1977-1980

Harold J. McMurtry
1972-1982, 1985

Phillip Hardeman
1981-1985

Thomas S. Nelms
1981-1982*

John W. (Bill) Kearns
1981-1985

T. Mack Blackburn
1983-1985*

Richard Vaughn
1985

Appendix A

Collin McDaniel

Frequently seen is the name Collin McDaniel, and its various spellings, in connection with the history of Brentwood. He was settled on his plantation, presently the site of Stonehenge Subdivision, from the earliest days of Williamson County. He operated an inn there, which he described as being on the main road to Natchez and New Orleans. For many years, he represented the Brentwood District on the County Court as well as serving as postmaster at the Good Spring Post Office.

In 1826, Collin McDaniel wrote a letter to his sister in Virginia. Your author has taken the liberty of paraphrasing and modernizing the original spelling and punctuation while at the same time trying to retain the flavor of the letter. So altered, the letter follows in part:

> Our misfortunes have been considerable since you saw us. Ten of our Negroes have died and the valuablest part of our stock, five of which were poisoned. We have however retained a compitancency sufficient to live independent, pay our debts and educate our children. We have educated our eldest children principally at a male and female academy of the most expensive kind.
>
> We have 11 childrem, five sons and six daughters. Mary Jane, our eldest, not married, remains with us. Her education is good and her intellectual powers of a superior order.
>
> Our second child Mosby, was a great soldier in the late war. He fought at the Battles of the Creek Nation and at New Orleans and the Seminole War. He was appointed a lieutenant of the 8th Regiment, U.S. Cavalry. He was ordered to New Orleans and the Bay of St. Louis where he

remained one or two years. He thereby imbided early in strong habits of dissipation and wickedness. At length he resigned and returned home. He possessed a heart filled with generosity, but he was careless of those appearances which more prudent men attend to. His better judgment had been impaired by a repetition of intemperence. His education was liberal and his intellectual powers good. He was taken from the stage of action on the 18th day of January last by a violent influenza which lasted him only two days. He was the following day interred in the narrow house of death. I am of the opinion that had he been as temperate as most young men, he might have yet been living.

Our third child Elizabeth Anne was married on the 5th day of December 1819 to Samuel C. Woolridge, Esquire, who is now and has been for several years past Treasurer of the State of Mississippi. He has a salary of 1,450 dollars per annum, an independent estate of a first rate family and character. He is a man of sobriety, talents and much politeness. His wife is a fine prudent and a sensible woman who has produced us four very fine grandchildren.

Our fourth Narcissa who visited her sister Woolridge at the seat of government, Mississippi, and was married to a member of the Assembly, a merchant and postmaster of Monitcello, Miss., a New York raised young man of a first rate family, and independent fortune and possessed a very superior understanding, a liberal education and truly a gentleman in every respect. She was shrewd, intelligent and very handsome, whose death was occasioned by the premature birth of her first child. After 10 days of indisposition of a slight fever, her husband, absent till the last two or three days, was sent for, who had for the first time left her since they were married and traveled from Monticello to Natchez a distance of 70 miles to receive his goods that were landing at that place. He arrived in a torrent of rain in the greatest distress and found her situation critical and awful. The mail had that moment arrived, which brought him a letter from me. He immediately carried it to her. She said is was her father's handwriting and requested him to open and read it. He did so. She listened and the language of her eyes appeared to understand every work perfectly. She was incapable of a reply of any kind and remained so till her death two or three days later. Her infant and herself were deposited in the same coffin of superior workmanship and afterwards in an elegant tomb.

Our fifth Alfred Washington aged 21 years a youth possessing talents superior to most men of his age, left us December last and resides at Washington six miles from Natchez. He is a clerk to the surveyor general of the public land south of Tennessee and deputy surveyor under the general government. He is engaged in a very profitable and respectable business, that of sectioning the public land and laying off the same into townships. His surveying will principally be in the Northern Boundary of Louisiana and on the Mississippi River. He is handsome, modest and unassuming, the best musician of flute or violin I ever saw of his age.

The sixth Marie Louisa, 19 years old August next, left us two years last month in company with her sister Woolridge who visited us with her little children, tarried a few months and returned home again. Maria was married at her residence, town of Jackson, seat of Government, Mississippi, to David W. Haley, a young man of high standing in Society. He is a most unexceptionable character for sobriety, industry, genuine merit and morality, who has for the last five years cleared upwards of 30 thousand dollars, clear, of all expense for transportation of the U.S. Mail from the Choctaw Nation to New Orleans, a distance of upwards of 400 miles. We expect them to visit us in a few weeks. Mr. Haley will then be on his way to Washington City to renew his contract. His wife will remain with us till he returns. They visited and remained in the City of New Orleans upwards of two months last winter. Maria is bright, genious, well educated, a superior talent for portrait painting.

Eliza Harriet, our seventh, aged 16 years, a very interesting intelligent girl who much resembles her deceased sister, will finish her education about the 20th and return home from the female Academy at Nashville.

The 8th and 9th are our twins Horatio and Charlotte. The latter of which is a smart girl aged 14 years. The former of which was a very smart child in his infancy. At the age of 7 or 8 he was long and violently afflicted with Typhus fever, which has ever since appeared to have much impaired his mind and understanding. We live in much hopes he will yet recover from the injury.

The 10th Robert Mosby is a handsome boy aged 9 years, wild, noisy and mischievous, industrious. I have had the fondest prediction for him from the earliest moments of his existence, a child who has so far possessed a genius of superior order. I believe he will if he lives to make a man be far superior to any of my name I ever saw.

The 11 William is a beautiful boy aged 6 years. His intellectual comes very little inferior to that of Robert.

It is highly probable that we shall never see each other again. If so, may we be prepared to meet in heaven. I have lived at my present residence from upwards of 22 years. I have served my country with others as a magistrate for the last 13 or 14 years. I am much healthier for the last 13 or 14 months than usual in consequence of having entirely declined from chewing tobacco from the use of which I received considerable injury after 40 years to use.

My wife retains a tolerable portion of health, carries her age well. My sons and myself all drink nothing stronger than water, for the last 23 or 24 years. I have had no spirits at all.

My greatest respects to all the children and family. Accept my dear my greatest wishes for your future and prosperity and happiness here and hereafter.

Collin McDaniel

Appendix B

Gone To Texas

The familiar sign "GTT" was tacked on many Middle Tennessee cabin doors in the 1830's and 1840's, indicating that the former resident had "gone to Texas." Indeed, Middle Tennessee was a crossroads to points south, west, and north. As lands began to open up, Middle Tennesseans moved into them. Some went to West Tennessee, Arkansas, Mississippi, Missouri, Indiana, and Illinois, but the haven seemed to be Texas.

Second generation natives of Brentwood went to Texas by the scores to find their fortunes. A few really did. When the Mexican War came along in the 1840's, every able-bodied male of enlistment age in the 15th District of Williamson County (now the City of Brentwood) is said to have enlisted in the army. They did so to go to Texas to protect their kinsmen who had settled there. This response to the call to arms during the Mexican War earned Tennessee the nickname "The Volunteer State."

One settler who went to Texas from Brentwood was Samuel Miles Frost, oldest son of Captain John Frost and his wife Rhoda Miles Frost. He left Brentwood and located in the San Antonio area of Texas in the 1840's. Family papers indicate that he corresponded regularly with his kinsmen in Brentwood.

In an overwhelming display of a mother's love for her first-born, Rhoda Miles Frost, when she was past the age of 60, rode horseback to Texas to see her son and his family. In 1855, she wrote a letter back to her youngest son, Sterling Brown Frost, who lived at the family farm in Brentwood. That letter follows in part:

Fort Bend County, Texas
April 17th, 1855
Dear Son & Daughter,

With gratitude to my great Redeemer I again resume my pen to inform you that I am in the injoyment of as good as I could expect in any country & do most ardently hope that these few lines may find you & your family in the injoyment of good health the greatest blessing of this life. S. M.'s wife has had another hard spell of sickness about a month ago. She rode to her Father's & was in feeble health & she took a verry fevear cough & coald & it apeard to settle on her lung & she has verry bad cough yet & cam verry near dying but she is recuperating slowly. Her youngest child is reighly a verry fine stout healthy looking boy. I thinke he will weigh betwean 25 & 30. He will bee a month oald the 22 of this mo & S. M. is one of the busyest men that you ever lave seen. Her son has been raised by hand. He drinks about half gallon of boiled milk a day & night fresh from the cows.

Rebeccas family are all well except Issac. He has chills & fever. She have had a hard time. She lives in a low flat place without a twig to break the wind on the north side of her house for about 5 mile with out a fence to her garden although she apears to bee in tolerable good spirits although labouring under dificultys she milks six or 7 cows & is trying to make som butter to sell.

Henry seemes to do tolerable well considering he has always, done as he pleases or did so when his father lived. He helps his Mother with the cows & takes good care of his horse & goes to school. Susan goes also & teacher says the boath of them learns verry fast.

We have had a verry coald winter & a verry backward spring & remarkable dry. S. M.'s crop was killed to the root of his corn & they planted 70 or 80 acres over again but S. M. is selling corn at hom at one per bushel, hauling to Hewston at one 15 or 25. He has made from to hundred & to.00 to 300 thousand this spring.

Rober Pollard is working at Oald Mr. Masons making 25 per month & is yet well pleased with the country if there was som of the Tennessee girls here he would like it much beter.

Dear Martha I am much gratified that you sent me some of the hair of the dear little ones that I can weap over but the are better of those that are gone. Take care of two you have left. Train up in the fear of the Lord for if we never met on this shores of time I hope to mete you at Gods right hand were parting will bee no more.

Please to give my best respects to all inquireing friends the 3 Mrs. Sneads & their familyes & aunt Jane Sconce & all inquireling friend please ask Susan Snead if her & the Major did receive a letter from me last fall.

Give my best respects to Mrs. Sprence & all your friends.

Dear M. E. F.

You spoke of my likeing to hear of work being done & do I do. If you can sell all you have to spare buy feathers you can sell them for 50 cts per pound. The cotton stocking I bought of Mrs. Spence I soald for 75 per pair. Peopel do not pretend to spin or weave. They buy all their clothing buy the goods cheaper than they can bee maid.

Respecting your Fathers serves in the Creek War he was one the first volentear in the horse company & I think belonge to Captain Shannons company. I think they started from hom the 2 September 1813 & redevoused at Huntsville under Gen Jackson & was in too engagments one at Toledo & I think the other at Talehatche & the men came near starving. The drew no ration for some time. I will refer you to C. P. Snead he was acainted with him.

As to your grandfathers death I think I can come verry near to the time if your Father had been living he would have bin 80 years oald the 27 of Jany past. I have frequently herd him say he was 8 yers oald when his father was killed in the revolution & it took place on the waters of Taepee Inoree or Tiger River. The war trying to storm a fort. I think he had a plaantaion in that neighborhood as his wife continued to live ther & had another husband & the O'Neall family raised the first four children & I have seen several of the second family. Receive my best wishes for your wellfare & believe me your ever well wishing Mother till death.

R. Frost

Please to tell John B. Copeland to pleas to pay Bets the 12 dollar he owed her.

Appendix C

The Nightclub Era

There was a time when Franklin Road was more well known for its night clubs than for its plantation homes. The 1930's and 1940's were the heyday of these clubs.

Brentwood's first tavern, McDaniel's, dates back to the 1800's and was located on Franklin Road, now the site of Stonehenge Subdivision. The cedar tree next to the highway stood in the yard of the tavern. Because there were no hotels, many taverns also provided lodging. In 1807, two travelers recorded that they stoped at McDaniel's Tavern, "a decent house, where we quartered the night." McDaniel's Tavern later became a stagecoach stop and post office.

In the recent past, Brentwood was the place where Nashvillians came to party. A large number of nightclubs was located here. The Palms Club, known far and wide as the finest club in the Nashville area, was in Brentwood proper, at the site of the current Exxon Station. Numerous Nashvillians have related that this club was of the highest quality, offering an evening of dining and dancing in pleasant surroundings.

The Stork Club was located on what is now Pewitt Drive, next door to Pewitt's Garage. The Pewitt family lived upstairs over their garage, and Barbara Campbell, daughter of the Emery Pewitts, recalls that Snooky Lanson would perform at the club and "sing her to sleep at night" when she was a child, as his voice carried from the club to their residence.

Several clubs, including the Stork Club, housed illegal slot machines, which meant that occasionally these clubs would be raided. To circumvent arrest, the owner of the Stork Club placed his slot machines on a dumbwaiter apparatus, so that when the club was raided he could drop the machines into the basement and hide them from the authorities.

The Ship A'Hoy was situated on Franklin Road at the site of what is now the Franklin Road Deli. Similarly the veterinary clinic on Franklin Road south of Wykle Road was formerly a nightclub called The Rendezvous.

The Owl was across the road from the Rendezvous on the west side of Franklin Road at the foot of Holly Tree Gap Hill. The foundation is still visible, but the building itself is gone. The Lucky Strike was at Moore's Lane and Franklin Road, now the site of Brentwood Rental. Nearer to Franklin, just beyond Berry's Chapel Road, The Greyhound was run for many years by "Daddy" Young. This night spot took its name from a pack of greyhounds kenneled there.

eAppendix D

Boy Scout Troop #1

Boy Scout Troop #1 of Brentwood dates back to 1910, the year of the founding of the Boy Scouts. The troop was organized by Curtis B. Haley in the basement of his Brentwood home. The founder of the Boy Scouts organization in America was Englishman Sir Robert Baden-Powell. He visited the Brentwood troop in 1912.

In 1911, Haley and two members of his scout troop were awarded medals for rescue work they did after a boating accident on Stones River. The presentation was made by President William Howard Taft at the Ryman Auditorium. The two boys who received the awards were James Avent and Carl Cooper.

As of this writing, Boy Scout Troop #1 has had only two scoutmasters, the founder Curtis B. Haley and Billy Jim Vaughn, who has been scoutmaster since 1935.

Index

A

Acklen, Adelicia Hayes — 26
Alfred, Sarah — 70
Allen, Owen — 121
Allison, A.A. — 101
American Ace — 116,117,123
Anderson, Arnold — 113
Anderson, John T. — 113
Arnold, Eddie — 124
Ashlawn — 26, 61, 75, 76, 121
Autry, Gene — 116
Avent, James — 152

B

Bachman, Henry R. — 29
Bailey, R.C. — 143
Bain, Thomas H. — 143
Baker, John — 20
Baker, William — 19
Barbara's House of Beauty — 128, 130
Battle of Franklin — 90, 96
Battle of Murfreesboro — 90
Battle of Nashville — 90
Beauregard, General — 87
Bell, David — 108
Bell, John — 107
Bell, Montgomery — 61, 75
Bell, Ray — 75
Benton, Thomas Hart — 105, 107
Blackburn, T. Mack — 143
Board of Zoning Appeals — 139
Bobo, Mrs. Dorothy Duffield — 113

Boiling Springs Academy — 92
Boiling Springs Mounds — 11
Boone, Daniel — 19
Boston — 125
Boxwood Hall — 72, 73
Boy Scout Troop #1 — 152
Bradford, Aleck — 109
Brentvale — 57, 82
Brentwood Baptist Church — 72
Brentwood Barber Shop — 128, 130
Brentwood Country Club — 14, 71
Brentwood Derby — 124
Brentwood Horse Show — 124
Brentwood, map of — 85
Brentwood United Methodist Church —
    68, 74, 84, 96-98
Bright, Irby — 124
Bright Hour Farm — 124
Brook, Cadi — 20
Brook's Chapel Road — 113
Bryan, Lewis C. — 98
Bryan, W. Allen III — 142
Burr, William — 98

C

Caldwell, Rogers — 124
Callendar, William — 76
Callendar Lane — 109
Campbell, Barbara — 130, 151
Cannon, Joshua — 94
Cannon, Lucy — 66
Carr, James A. — 113
Carr, William M. — 113
Carmack, Daniel — 108

Carnton Association — 84
Carondelet Subdivision — 25, 108
Carpenter, Morton — 109
Carter, Eliza — 101
Castleman, Eliza — 101
Castleman, Louis — 101
Century Oak — 37, 77, 78, 87, 121
Chapel Hill — 87
Chartier, Martin — 19
Cherokee — 11, 17
Chickamauga — 11, 17
Chickasaw — 11, 17
Chidlow, Mrs. Rita Johnson — 130
Chocktaw — 17
Christmas, Emeline — 26
Christmas, Mary Ann Smith — 61
Christmas, Richard — 26, 61, 75
Church Street — 30
Church Street East — 96, 104, 109
City Manager — 139
Civil District, 15th — 30
Civil War — 35, 72, 73, 81, 82, 86-91
Clare, Major William — 96
Clark, Dr. W.M. — 30
Cleland, Charles T. — 113
Clover Lawn — 79, 82, 121
Cloverland Drive — 22, 109
Cloverland Estates — 22
Cockrill, John — 79
Coffey, John — 107
Concord Road — 16, 66, 70, 82, 90, 93, 94,
    106, 109
Cooper, Carl — 152
Cotton, T.M. — 102
Cotton Port — 59, 67

Cox, N.N. — 79
Creek — 23, 58
Critchlow, Adeline — 101
Critchlow, J.B. — 101
Crockett, Major Andrew — 36, 53, 79, 80
Crockett, Emily — 71
Crockett, Hillary — 113
Crockett, James — 70, 71
Crockett, Joseph — 50
Crockett, Polly — 80
Crockett, Samuel — 36, 80
Crockett Road — 87
Crockett Springs — 50, 80
Cullum, Reverend Jeremiah — 103
Cumberland Compact — 25
Cumberland River — 27
Cumberland University — 92

D

Daniel, Robert — 104
David Lipscomb College — 76
Davis, Judith Robertson Owen — 55
Davis, William — 30, 55, 74
DeGraffenreid Site — 14, 15
Del Rio Pike — 14
Derryberry, Marshall — 121
DeSoto, Hernando — 18, 19, 23
Devon Farm — 28
Donelson, John — 21
Dotson, Richard — 113
Dow, Lorenzo — 94
Drake, D.L. — 96
Duffield, Alva E. — 113
Dyer, Arthur J. — 72, 121

E

Eaton's Station — 24
Edmondson, Henry — 104
Edmondson, John — 32, 108
Edmondson, Thenia — 104
Edmondson, Major Thomas — 105
Edmondson Pike — 66, 68, 109
Edmunds, Addison L. — 113
Edney, Levin — 99
Eggert, Edwin C. — 124
Ehresman, Marie Little — 65
Emanuel, Victor — 116
Evans, Lawrence — 102
Evans, Thomas — 70
Exxon Station, Pewitt's — 128-129, 130

F

Fanning, Tolbert — 93
fences, stone — 30, 64
Fewkes, E.W. — 14
Fewkes Site — 14
Forrest, Nathan Bedford — 87, 91
Forge Seat — 36, 80

Forsythe, Robert C. — 100
Fort Donelson — 86
Fort Henry — 86
Fort Nashboro — 22, 25, 65
Foster, William L. — 113
Foxview — 82
Frank, Mrs. Richard — 113
Franklin — 14, 84, 87, 88, 106
Franklin Interurban Railroad — 109
Franklin Road — 29, 30, 70, 89, 90, 91, 105, 127, 128, 129
Franklin Turnpike Company — 107
French Lick — 20
Frost, Captain John — 59, 67, 68
Frost, John — 68, 148
Frost, Jonathan — 68
Frost, Mary Benson — 68
Frost, Rhoda Miles — 59, 67, 148-150
Frost, Samuel Miles — 148
Frost, Sterling Brown — 96, 108
Frost Cemetery — 103
Fulcher, Richard — 29
Funkhouser, Christopher — 70
Furlough, Aaron — 129

G

Gallatin — 86
Gant, B.R. — 98
Gardner, Frank G. — 102
Gasser, Frank — 79, 83, 121
Goff, Norrie — 116
Gooch, Beverly R. — 128
Gooch, John B. — 127
Gooch Television Service — 127-128
Good Spring Post Office — 112
Gordon, Thomas — 20
Grand Ole Opry — 127
Granny White Pike — 91, 107
Green, A.L.P. — 98
Green, Jack — 143
Greenbriar — 125
Green Pastures — 63, 73, 121, 125
Greer, Kate Jones — 71
Grundy, Felix — 96, 107

H

Hadley, Denny Porterfield — 26, 63, 73, 108
Hadley, Elizabeth — 26, 63, 73
Hadley, Joshua — 73
Hadley, Mary — 96
Hadley, William — 96
Hadleywood, 63, 73
Hair Studio, the — 130
Haley, Curtis B. — 152
Hall, James H. M. — 113
Hanner, John W. — 98
Hardeman, Philip — 143
Hardeman, Susannah Perkins — 81

Harding, William Giles — 81
Hardscuffle Road — 96, 104, 109, 129
Harpeth Hills Hunt Club — 124
Harpeth River — 27
Harpeth Turnpike — 30, 82, 107, 108
Harriman, Rizerdorf — 113
Harris, Reuben E. — 142
Hartsville — 86
Hayes, Elizabeth — 72
Hayes, Emily McGavock — 72
Hayes, McGavock — 72, 97
Hayes, Oliver Bliss — 26
Hayes, Oliver Bliss Jr. — 72
Hearthstone Subdivision — 70
Henley, Mr. and Mrs. Jesse — 26
Herbert, George — 31
Herbert, George Washington Charmichael — 19
Herbert, John — 68
Herbert, Judith — 83
Herbert, Richard — 68
Herbert, Robert Nathaniel — 69, 108
Herbert, Robert Nathaniel Jr. — 68
Hicks, Edward W. — 27
Hightower, Richard — 25, 108
Hightower, Sarah Clemmons — 26
Hildebrand, Miriam Fly — 65
Hill, Green — 66, 94
Hill, Joshua Cannon — 66
Hillsboro Hounds — 125
Hogan, Humphrey — 20
Holly Tree Gap — 89, 91, 105
Holmes, T. — 96
Holt, Elizabeth — 104
Holt, Isabella Hardeman — 83
Holt, John — 83
Holt, John Page — 83
Holt, O'Dell — 84
Holt, Thomas — 83
Holt, Will — 84
Holt, William — 104
Hood, General John Bell — 78, 86, 90, 96
Horton, A.W. — 101
Horton, Joshua — 19
Houghland, Calvin Jr. — 124
Houghland, Mason — 121, 125
Houston, Sam — 76, 77
Howell, Charles — 70
Howell, Charles A. III — 70
Hubbard, George Whipple — 82
Huff, Glenn — 129-130
Huff, Mike — 130
Huff's Market — 128, 129-130
Humphries, J.P. — 30
Humphries, Randolph — 65
Hunt, Gersham — 66, 67
Hunt, Henry — 104
Hunt, Jonathan — 66
Hunt, Lon — 104
Hunt, Sarah Orton — 67
Hunt, William Carroll — 67

I

Indian Point Subdivision — 84
Indians — 11-17
Inglehame — 77, 121
Iroquois Steeplechase — 122-123
Irvin, General Robert — 35, 70
Isola Bella — 78, 121

J

Jackson, General Andrew — 58, 80, 81, 107
Jackson Highway — 105
Johnson, Andrew — 86
Johnson, Bob — 104
Johnson Chapel — 96, 99
Johnston, James — 78, 108
Johnston, Narcissa Merritt — 78
Johnstone, Major John — 99
Johnstone, Matthew — 99
Jones, Floyd W. — 127
Jones, Mary Sneed — 63, 82, 112
Joslin, Barry — 24

K

Kearns, John W. — 143
Kelly Road — 14
Kelley, David C. — 98
Kennedy, T.P. — 121
Knox-Crockett House — 53, 79

L

L & N Railroad — 30
Lamb, Walter — 113
Lanson, Snooky — 151
LaSalle — 19
Lawrence, Frank — 100
Lazenby, John — 101
Lazenby, Sarah — 101
Lebanon — 86
Leeds, Daniel Lake — 113, 127
Leeds Store — 127
Leiper Grant — 25, 75
Leiper, Captain James — 25, 70, 73, 75
Leiper, Sarah Jane — 25, 73
Leiper, Susan Drake — 25
Lewisburg Pike — 14, 15
Liberty Hill — 65
Liberty Methodist Church — 65, 94, 95
Liberty Pike — 89
Library Board — 139
Lipscomb, David — 76, 103
Lipscomb, William — 93
Lipscomb Elementary School — 93
Little, Robert Milton — 67
Little, T. Vance — 90
Little, William Robert — 66
Little Harpeth River — 14, 27, 70, 77

Little Harpeth Valley — 12
Louisville and Nashville Railroad Company
    — 108

M

Maloney, Mr. and Mrs. Albert — 71
Mansker, Casper — 20
Maple Grove Farm — 121
Maple Lawn — 33, 79
Marshall, Lucy Ann — 37, 77
Martin, Dr. W.W. — 72
Maryland Farms — 116-120, 123, 124
Maryland Manor — 117
Maury, Matthew Fontaine — 107
Mayfield — 58
Mayfield Station — 67, 109
Mayfield, George — 25, 58
Mayfield, James — 24
Mayfield, Dr. Southerland Shannon — 24,
    25, 58
Mayfield, William — 25
Mayor, the — 139
McClanahan, Mrs. Ophelia — 100
McClendon, Dennis — 32
McCord, Doc — 109
McCord, William H. — 143
McCrory House — 41, 83
McCrory, Thomas — 41, 83, 99
McDaniel, Collin — 108, 144-147
McFerrin, J.B. — 101
McGavock, Cynthia — 72
McGavock, David — 71
McGavock, Lysander — 71, 72
McMurray, Dr. William J. — 87, 91
McMurtry, Harold J. — 143
McNish, Horatio — 29, 30
Meadow Lake Subdivision — 14, 109
Midway — 71, 72
Midyett, Thomas E. Jr. — 142
Mill Creek — 16, 90
Mizell, Andrew — 76
Mizell, Lucy Merrill — 76
Mooney, W. — 98
Moore, Eleanor Irvin — 70, 94
Moore, Mr. and Mrs. Hugh C. Sr. — 96
Moore, Hugh Campbell — 71
Moore, James — 70, 94
Moore, Robert Irvin — 29, 30, 35, 71
Moore, Robert Irvin IV — 71
Moore, Ruth — 71
Moore's Lane — 11, 79, 92
Mooreland — 35, 70, 71, 91, 96
Morel, Junius — 100
Morgan, Frank — 113
Morgan, George W. — 102
Morris, Billy — 101
Mound Builders — 14, 15, 17, 18
Mt. Lebanon Missionary Baptist Church —
    104

Mountview — 55, 74, 121
Murfreesboro — 87

N

Nashville and Decatur Railroad Company
    — 108
Natchez Trace — 14
Nelms, Thomas S. — 143
Nelson, General William — 77
Newland, William P. — 113
Noble, Albert H. — 128
Noble, Glenn — 50, 80, 113, 128
Noble's Restaurant — 128
Noel, Mr. and Mrs. Oscar — 71
Nolensville — 86, 89
North, Reverend Henry — 101

O

Oden, H. — 96
Oden, Rebecca — 70
Oden, Marion — 113, 128
Oden, Mary Sophronia — 70
Oden, Solomon — 69
Oden, Solomon Fletcher — 69
Oden, Tom — 64, 82
Odyssey Salon — 128
Old Hickory Boulevard — 124
Old Natchez Trace — 27
Old Smyrna Road — 15, 19, 30, 67, 68,
    69, 80, 81, 82, 103, 108, 112
Oman, Mr. and Mrs. John — 78, 121
Oman, Mr. and Mrs. Stirton — 61, 76,
    121
Orchid Lounge — 151
Owen, Miss Callie Lillie — 80, 81
Owen, Everett — 74, 108
Owen, Jabez — 39, 79, 80
Owen, Jane Hightower — 33, 79
Owen, Judith Robertson — 74
Owen, Nathan — 33, 79, 108
Owen, Peter — 108
Owen, Robert Rowland — 82
Owens, Bob — 104
Owens, Stephen — 104
Owen's Chapel Church of Christ — 103
Owen-Primm House — 39, 79
Owl Creek — 16
Owl Creek Site — 16

P

Page, Elmira — 83
Parker, Malcolm — 16
Pearson, Harry — 124
Perkins, Bethenia — 81
Perkins, Charles — 104
Perkins, Constantine — 45
Perkins, Nicholas Tate — 81

Perkins, Thomas Harden — 81
Pewitt, Emery — 128, 129, 130, 142, 151
Pewitt, Luther — 128
Peyton, Ephraim — 22
Phillips, Jesse H. — 108
Pitts, Fountain E. — 98
Pitts, J.J. — 101
Planning Commission — 139
Plaxico, Charles — 121
Pointer, Solomon — 104
post office — 64, 109-113
Potter, Edward — 78, 117, 121, 125
Puryear, William — 121

Q

Quintard, Reverend Charles — 96

R

Ragsdale, Walter D. — 113
Ransom, R.P. — 98
Ravenswood — 76
Reams, Robert — 96
Redd, James T. — 142
Redmon, Mrs. Mae J. — 113
Reed, James M. — 112
Reelfoot Lake — 70
Renegar, Mr. and Mrs. G.W. — 80
Renegar, Mary Sue Owen — 81
Riggs, Adam S. — 98
Robards, William L. — 108
Robertson, Colonel James — 21, 23, 25
Robertson Academy — 124
Robinson, Bob — 142
Rozell, Ashley B. — 74
Rutledge, Bobby — 130

S

Saddlewood Subdivision — 22
Sang Yi — 130
Sawyer, John — 113
Schofield, John M. — 90
Schwab family — 82
Seratoga Hills Subdivision — 66
Sewell, Benjamin — 94
Sharp, Vernon — 77, 121
Shawnee — 11, 16, 19
Sheler, Charles R. — 113
Shell Station, Rhea Little's — 109
Shiloh — 87
Shockley, Jeff — 109
Simpson, George W. — 113
Simpson, John N. — 113
Sister Cities Board — 140

Sloan, John Jr. — 142
Sloan, John Sr. — 121, 125
Smith, Alexander — 25, 26, 30, 73, 75
Smith, Bob — 124
Smith, Colonel James — 19
Smith, Mary Emeline — 75
Smith, Mr. and Mrs. Reece — 77
Smith, Robert — 25
Smith, Sarah Clemmons — 25
Smith, Sarah Jane Leiper — 73, 75
Smyrna Church — 96, 103-104
Sneed, Alexander Ewing — 82
Sneed, Bethenia Harden Perkins — 46, 80, 81
Sneed, Cornelia — 104
Sneed, Constantine Perkins — 81
Sneed, Constantine Perkins Jr. — 82
Sneed, James — 46, 57, 64, 80, 81, 82
Sneed, James Hardeman — 82
Sneed, Martha Nance — 81
Sneed, Mary DeLoach — 81
Sneed, Mary Hunt — 104
Sneed, Robert Scales — 82
Sneed, Jim P. — 104
Sneed, Susannah Hardeman — 45
Sneed, Dr. William J. — 82
Sneed, William L. — 108
Sneed, William Temple — 57, 82
Sneed, Zachariah — 81
Sneed Acres — 46, 81
South Harpeth River — 27
Spectator, The — 28
Spires, Moses — 94
Split Log Road — 77
Spring Hill — 90
Stahlman, James — 125
Standfield, Spivey — 108
Stanwyck, Barbara — 116
Star Market — 128, 130
Stone, Uriah — 19, 20
Stonehenge Subdivision — 112, 151
Stones River — 19
Stubblefield, Mrs. Sam M. — 78
Sweeney, Brian Joe — 139, 142

T

Taverns — 151-152
Tennessee Historical Society — 28
Thompson, Larry — 104
Thompson Station — 87, 88
Thornton, Guilford F. — 143
Thurso — 78, 121
Tilford, J.M. Crown — 92
Traveler's Rest — 14, 96
Traveler's Rest Motel — 128
Troxler, Mrs. Yvonne — 130
Tucker, Catherine — 101
Tucker, Frances — 101
Tucker, Harvey — 101

Tucker, Mary — 101
Tucker, R.C. — 102
Tucker, Rachel — 101
Tucker, Stephen — 96
Tucker, Susan — 101
Tulloss, Major John E. — 77
Turrentine, Rev. A.D. — 104

V

Valley View Farm — 64, 82
Van Buren, Martin — 107
Vaughn, Billy Jim — 152
Vaughn, Richard — 143

W

Waller, Pierce — 108
Waller, Thenia — 104
Walters, Laban — 108
Ward, J. Truman — 116, 120, 123
Ward, Jim — 120, 123
Ward, Mary — 116
Wautauga Settlement — 17
Weiland, Raymond L. — 143
West Harpeth River — 27
White, Raymond — 83
Wildview — 87
Wildwood — 84
Wilkins, Rob — 104
Williams, James T. — 113
Williams, Rob — 104
Williams, Sallie — 104
Williams, Turner — 108
Wilson, Charles P. — 75, 121
Wilson, Emeline — 76
Wilson, James Hazard — 76, 107
Wilson, James Hazard II — 37, 77
Wilson, James Hazard III — 77
Wilson, Samuel — 37, 76
Wilson Pike — 15, 25, 30, 70, 76, 77, 79, 82, 89, 107-108, 112, 129
Wilson Pike Circle — 130
Windy Hill — 45, 81
Winstead Hill — 90
Witherspoon, Charles Jr. — 84
Witherspoon, Kate Holt — 84
WLAC Radio Station — 116
WSM Radio Station — 129
WSM Radio Tower — 109

Z

Zellner, Henry — 76
Zellner, James Jr. — 76
Zellner, Lucy — 76
Zollicoffer, General Felix — 69, 77
Zollicoffer, Virginia — 77

About the Author

Thomas Vance Little, a Brentwood attorney, is a graduate of Vanderbilt University and is a member of the American Bar Association, the Tennessee Bar Association, and the Nashville Bar Association. He is presently associated with Gordon, Bottorff, Waters, and Little, a Brentwood law firm. Mr. Little is a member of the Tennessee Historical Society, the Williamson County Historical Society, the Heritage Foundation of Franklin and Williamson County, the Carnton Association, the Tennessee State Museum Association, the Association for the Preservation of Tennessee Antiquities, the Natchez Trace Parkway Association, the Sons of Confederate Veterans, and the Sons of the American Revolution. His lifelong residency in Williamson County plus his intense interest and efforts related to the history of Brentwood provide him with unique qualifications to capture the rare and significant events related to the history of Brentwood.

About the Photographer

Doug H. Brachey, a native Nashvillian, has been a resident of Williamson County for 12 years. He is a graduate of Middle Tennessee State University and is owner of Doug Brachey Photography of Brentwood.

Mr. Brachey has lived in Brentwood for two years with his wife, Dawn, and their three children, Todd, Troy, and Meghan.